Advertising and Sales Promotion

An Indian Perspective

Advertising and Sales Promotion

An Indian Perspective

V.S. Padmanabhan

Freelance Consultant in
Public Relations

❃

H.S. Murthy

Professor & HOD
Management Studies
City College, Bengaluru

Ane Books Pvt. Ltd.

New Delhi ♦ Chennai

Advertising and Sales Promotion: An Indian Perspective

V.S. Padmanabhan and H.S. Murthy

Published by

Ane Books Pvt. Ltd.

4821, Parwana Bhawan, 1st Floor, 24 Ansari Road, Darya Ganj,
New Delhi - 110 002, Tel.: +91(011) 23276843-44, Fax: +91(011) 23276863
e-mail: kapoor@anebooks.com, Website: www.anebooks.com

Branch Office :

- Avantika Niwas, 1st Floor, 19 Doraiswamy Road, T. Nagar,
  Chennai - 600 017, Tel.: +91(044) 28141554, 28141209
  e-mail: anebookschennai@gmail.com, rathinam@anebooks.com

ISBN : 978-81-9083-228-1

Printed at : Sagar Colorscan, New Delhi.

IIMB

तेजस्वि नावधीतमस्तु

Foreword

Advertising and Sales Promotion is one of the most important marketing functions. The balancing of pull and push has been both, a practitioners nightmare and delight. For academics, it is much easier to pontificate. Here are two practitioners turned academics, who have put together the concepts in a simple and lucid manner, illustrated the concepts with wonderful examples, thereby facilitating the learning process.

There are many books on the subject by both, foreign and Indian authors. However, this book by Shri Murthy and Shri Padmanabhan stands out in terms of integrating the subject with the latest thinking in marketing and beautifully balancing the concepts with practice.

Happy learning.

Mithileshwar Jha
Professor of Marketing
Indian Institute of Management
Bengaluru

Preface

Until the time free India's Industrial Policy resolution was announced, textbooks on advertising started off with a debate—Is Advertising an art of science? The question never got resolved.

The advent of Marketing as an advanced management subject of study, free economy, pace of innovations, new products and services, intense competition, higher standard of living and economic growth has seen a paradigm shift in this area. No longer do we ask questions like is advertising an art or science. It has become an industry and today develops/uses solutions and strategies in totality as "Integrated Marketing Communications." Every ingredient of this contemporary discipline—singly and together—is a driving force behind the global competitive, free economy.

Viewed from outside, this industry or profession would appear to be glamorous. May be there is just a grain of truth in this. However, the person working in this industry would confess it is hard and harder work all the way. The solving of problems is challenging and no two time frames or situations are alike. There is constant change.

There is demand for people of excellence in every facet of this industry. The advertiser, the advertising consultancy, the numerous and complex media, the mind blogging number of allied services, all need people who are specialists who can lead and win.

The top management person or the student of management and marketing or anyone wanting to enter any facet of this industry neeeds thorough knowledge and understanding and this is crucial when one realises the market for goods and services is a "jungle" demanding strategies and ammunition to stay on top.

This book educates the aspirant and equally the top management. It opens the door for further studies and specialisation in marketing communications and areas allied to the business as also in innovative media, strategies and more.

The authors believe their efforts would help the growth of Indian expertise not only in India but also rest of the world.

Our thanks and appreciation to the editorial team of Ane Books Pvt. Ltd., for the excellent work done.

Contents

1

Introduction

1

Introduction

The 21st Century brought with it the phenomena of globalisation and information and technology which changed the world forever. The world has become a global village and people can share knowledge and information regardless of national boundaries. This new era is replete with new exciting opportunities and challenges for businesses as they have to compete globally as well as take care of local sensibilities. Advertising and sales promotion is the tool which helps the companies to reach their target customers.

As a specialised business, advertising originated in England and developed into a subject of study and application in the US. The term used hereafter "advertising" should be taken as inclusive of sales promotion and marketing communications. Both advertising and sales promotion are essentially economic activities and belong to the "information" business.

Indian Advertising Industry

The Indian advertising industry has evolved from a small business to a full-fledged service industry. It has emerged as one of the major industries and tertiary sectors and has broadened its horizons, be it the creative aspect, the capital or the number of personnel employed. Indian advertising industry in very little time span has carved a niche for itself, which is noteworthy. Indian advertising with an estimated turnover of Rs13,200 crore has made jaws drop and set eyeballs gazing with some astonishing pieces of work that it has given in the recent past. The creative minds in Indian advertising have come up with some mind-boggling concepts and work that can be termed as masterpieces in the field of advertising. Advertising agencies in the country too have taken a leap forward. They have come a long way from being small and medium–sized industries to becoming well known brands in the business. Mudra, Ogilvy and Mather (O&M),Low Lintas, J Walter Thomson (JWT), Mcann Ericsonn, Rediffussion, Leo Burnett are some of the top agencies of the country. Indian economy is booming and the market is on a continuous trail of expansion. Businesses are looking up to advertising as a powerful tool to cash in on lucrative business opportunities.

Indian advertising today handles both national and international business. This is primarily because the industry offers a host of services to its clients—everything from start to finish, from client servicing, media planning, media buying, creative conceptualisation, pre-and post-campaign analysis, market research, marketing, branding, rural marketing, event management, retail promotion, sponsorship, and public relation services. Keeping in mind the current pace at which the Indian advertising industry is moving, the industry is expected to witness a major boom in the times ahead and be a major contributor to the GDP.

Today none of us can escape the onslaught of advertising in our daily life. You pick up the morning newspaper and find more advertisement than news. You switch on the radio and are forced to listen to the ad jingles along with your favourite songs. Watching TV is not easy either as all programmers have more than necessary commercial breaks. Even when browsing the Internet ads keep popping up to catch your attention. But we should remember that all the information and entertainment reaches us because of the revenue advertising generates.

Advertising today has a key role to play in the economy. It helps to stimulate demand, introduce new products, reach potential customers who cannot be reached by salesmen etc.

Advertising is one of the many components of the promotion mix. Advertising is defined as "any paid form of non-personal communication for a product or service by an identified sponsor". Promotion mix is in turn an integral part of the marketing programme. Marketing programme uses a mix of marketing strategies which combines elements of product, price, place (distribution channel), and promotion. Promotional strategy uses a combination of promotional activities—termed as promotion mix.

Fig. 1.1: On television commercial breaks are frequent phenomena

The Marketing Mix

Marketing facilitates exchange of products and services for a price. These products and services are offered after analysing the needs and wants of the consumers. Having developed the product/service the marketer works out a price which is affordable to the customer, remunerative to the organisation and competitive.

The products/services offered must be made available to the customer at a convenient point of purchase. This is done through distribution channels, which can be as simple as direct marketing involving only the marketer and the customer. Or it can be a complex multilevel channel usually found in marketing of Fast Moving Consumer Goods (FMCG). The distribution strategy depends on the nature of the goods, spread of the consumers, buying habits etc.

Promotion is the last P of the four traditional Ps of marketing. No matter how good the product is, and irrespective of good pricing and distribution, the consumer will not buy it in the absence of awareness of its existence. We examine the role of promotion in the marketing mix in this chapter.

Some marketers have extended four Ps to six Ps to include packaging and people. However, since the traditional model of marketing mix includes this aspect, we have not mentioned it separately. And the subject of our further discussion will be promotion.

Traditionally marketing practitioners have focused on advertising, sales promotion, personal selling and direct marketing as activities of promotion. The modern thinking is that right from advertising to a simple letter written to a candidate for an interview is marketing communication.

Here our focus will be on all activities that lead to marketing communication. Consumer perception about a company's product/service is based on advertising, pricing, packaging, direct marketing efforts, encounter with salesman of the company, point of purchase, display of hoardings, and type of store where the product is sold. Integrated marketing communication programme synthesises all the activities of promotion in a manner that the consumer receives consistent and unified image of the product of the company.

The Promotional Mix (the Communication Mix): Tools For Integrated Marketing Communication

Traditionally the promotional mix has used a communication plan including advertising, sales promotion, publicity/public relations and personal selling. However, the modified new version of promotion mix also includes direct marketing and interactive media such as Internet (Fig. 1.2).

Fig. 1.2: The Promotion Mix

As mentioned earlier, advertising is defined as any paid form of non-personal communication for a product/service, by an identified sponsor.

The paid part of the definition indicates that the space/time is bought. Non-personal aspect refers to mass media of communication including broadcast media (TV, radio) or print media (newspapers, magazines, catalogues etc.). Since the communication is non-personal the task of advertising brings complexities in the process of communication as the message must be interpreted as planned by the advertiser. And of course advertising must evoke responses which lead to sales.

Advertising is probably the most important element of the promotion mix. The reasons are its ability to reach masses dispersed geographically at a very low per prospect contact cost.

Advertising is widely used in creating brand personality/brand image which enables consumers to choose a brand from a market where several brands exist. "The complete Man" image of Raymond suiting has been created over several decades, the beauty soap LUX has been deeply etched as a toilet soap which reminds common consumers of the beauty of the likes of Aishwarya Rai, Madhuri Dixit, Hema Malini, Meena Kumari, of course each one relevant to a different generation. Boost uses cricket master Sachin Tendulkar while Amitabh Bachchan endorses many everyday products.

DIRECT MARKETING is that element of promotion mix through which the company directly communicates with the prospective customer to get a favourable response. Direct marketing involves direct selling, telemarketing and direct response ads through the Internet, direct mail, and various broadcast and print media. Readers' Digest has been very successful in selling subscription. The British Institute which sells various educational programmes has used this route over the last few years. In India, Burlington has catalogue shopping which has been also a successful business model. Many credit card companies, hotels, resorts use telemarketing to promote their products. Maruti Udyog uses direct mailers to promote service after sales business.

Interactive/Internet Marketing

With the changes in technology, our ways of communicating and doing business have also changed. Interactive marketing is the mantra of the new millennium. Interactive media, such as Internet, has in recent times become a new way of advertising. It is not only the new IT generation but also the brick and mortar generation which is surfing on the information highway. Many businesses have built websites which are visited by Internet users. Other interactive media include—CD-ROM, kiosks and interactive television.

SALES PROMOTION is one of the oldest forms of promotion. Many brands in the past have adopted unconventional methods of sales promotion. A detergent launched in late 60s by Sarabhai group built its brand equity through sales promotion—brand Sway. A free bucket was offered with every purchase of 5 Kg Sway detergent. This sales promotion supported by point of purchase material was a runaway success.

Sales Promotion is of two kinds. The first one directed to the consumer (consumer oriented), while the second one is directed to the trade (trade oriented).

Consumer oriented sales promotion activities are targeted at ultimate consumers. The objective of these consumer promotions is to counter competition, introduce new products, induce trials, retain loyal customers, liquidate old stocks etc. The promotions take the form of discount coupons, pack price-off, consumer contests, scratch and win a prize, trade empty packs for discounts on next purchase, sampling, lottery(sweepstake). All these methods result in short-term sales gain.

Trade oriented sales promotion activities are for the benefit of the channel partners. These include display contests, mystery consumer campaign. Lottery, price deals, promotional and merchandising allowances, trade shows, get-togethers, etc. The objectives are to make the channel partners stock more of the company products, focus on company brands, actively promote company brand to consumers, provide more shelf space to company brands, use effectively promotional aids provided by the company, display company products at vantage points to attract the attention of customers visiting the shop, create favourable opinion about the company.

PUBLICITY In recent times (early 2010), however, media has been accused of "advertorials" which constitute editorially written and published advertisements. This ploy was used at elections and has drawn considerable criticism as "unethical". It refers to impersonal communications regarding organisation, product, service etc., which is not directly paid for or run under an identified sponsorship. It comes as an editorial, news report/story, and announcement. A company does not pay for this coverage or claims ownership of the news. However the company may use tactics to ensure favourable coverage of the company, products and its activities.

Word of mouth publicity: Many satisfied customers unwittingly become brand ambassadors. While shopping costly products such as refrigerators, television, consumers ask the present brand owners about the performance of the brand. If the customer is satisfied with the brand he will recommend it to others. This method of promotion is called 'word of mouth publicity'. Word of mouth publicity can be either positive or negative.

One singular advantage of publicity is that it has more credibility than advertising. The other advantage is that cost of publicity (hidden cost) is lower than promotional aids. Disadvantage of publicity is that it is not necessarily under control of the company and therefore the communication can be unpredictable. Soft drink Coca-Cola got negative publicity for destroying water table in a village in Kerala. Cadbury sometime back got adverse publicity after worms were reported to be found in its confectionary. These news items are published without consulting the company and may result in immense damage to brand equity. On the other hand, ethical practices of a company reported in the Press result in favourable view of the company by consumers.

PUBLIC RELATIONS is an organised method by the organisation to ensure favourable opinion about the company and its products. It involves planning and distribution of information to influence and change the attitudes of all those who interact with the company.

Public relations uses tools including corporate advertising campaigns, media relations, publications, direct mailers, fund-raising for community activities, sponsoring sports activities, offering education scholarships, maintaining parks etc. All these enhance the image of the company in the eyes of the public. Public Relation specialist companies offer services to those organisations which do not have in-house Public Relation facilities.

PERSONAL SELLING is the final element of promotion-mix. Personal selling involves direct person to person contact for selling of a product or a service. Unlike advertising there is a personal interaction with the potential customer providing scope for customising a sales pitch, overcoming objections etc. The message can be modified according to the type of customer. A feedback is immediate and can be used to change the presentation to suit the customer.

Compared to advertising personal selling is expensive. It is more suitable for high value products such as consumer durables or industrial products. Personal selling plays a key role in managing distribution channels in marketing of consumer products.

Summary

Advertising has a very important role to play in our life. It helps us make choices in our consumption of products and services. On the macro level advertising stimulates the economy by increasing demand for products, it increases competition and in turn offers quality product at reasonable prices to the consumers.

Promotional mix is made up of advertising; direct marketing, interactive/Internet marketing, sales promotion, publicity, public relation and personal selling. The choice of these components and the mix of these depend on how the company wants to promote the product.

Keywords

- Global Village
- Internet Marketing
- Integrated Marketing
- Communication Mix
- Personal Selling
- Channel Partners
- Advertising
- Direct Marketing
- Promotion Mix
- Publicity
- Brand Personality
- Interactive Marketing
- Sales Promotion
- Marketing Mix
- Public Relations
- Brand Image

Discussion Questions

1. What is the role of advertising in our life?
2. How does advertising impact the economy?

2

Before the Market Economy

2

Before the Market Economy

Early economic theory mentions Land, Labour and Capital as the three components of economy and looking at this theory, one realises that it reflects what was really happening at that period of time in history. That was an era of colonising. England had vast empires and so had France and other countries. The Capital was provided by the settlers, the labour were the local people in the colonies and African tribes taken to America as slaves or contract labour from India. The land was what the colonists occupied. The produce included everything from sugar, rubber, food grains, cotton, poppy, spices etc. Even after America became a free country and abolished slavery, the theory did not change.

The Nazis started their biggest colonising adventure via World War II and the colonial countries of Britain, France etc., fought to retain their colonies and their own nations. At the end of the War, what we witnessed was the opposite of colonising. The world now accepted that all were equals and every nation could administer itself. Thus, several new countries became free but not necessarily their wealth.

The most significant outcome of this end of all Wars as World War II is called, is in the field of technology. This needs no elaboration since we are already in a seamless one world-village. Another aspect is education that includes the Marketing discipline.

India

India was a country of many princely states but with a civilisation more than 15,000 years old and global trading/cultural contacts. The British came to India via the East India Trading Company but this turned out to be the harbinger of colonising India—in competition with the French, Dutch, Portuguese and others British managed to conquer whole of India. We became a supplier of raw material and cheap labour. Side by side, we became a large and protected market for British goods.

Until recently most history books written by British authors praised colonial rulers and suppressed truth. However, recently new books and doctorial dissertations have appeared, such as **Directions in Development, Late Victorian Holocausts** (by Mike Davis) and also observations by people like Digby who chronicled the famine in Madras (1876) during the British Rule. Up to 29 million Indians died despite surplus crops. The Governor General, Lord Lytton, exported a record 320,000 tonnes of wheat to England. By an official order any aid to the starving was banned. Despite famine, taxes were collected to fund the Afghan campaign. Later, in Oudh and Punjab, despite record harvests, exports were undertaken at the cost of some 1.25 million people who died of starvation. These reveal the extent of exploitation.

Managing Colonial Economy

These books reveal interesting facts, for example 60% of the World's GDP in 1790 was shared by China (31%) and India (29%). In 1790, 30% of India's income was from non-agricultural activities, such as spinning, textiles, industrial goods including ship building. By 1890, India's share in the world GDP was down to 11% (China's too down to 13%). Our rulers systematically destroyed our economic activities, throwing up a large class of landless proletariat. Discriminatory tariffs and transport rates killed off Indian producers of industrial goods.

Millions of acres used for growing crops were converted to cultivate poppy or (for export to the US during years of high prices there) cotton etc.

Indian money was diverted to Britain's Afghan wars, Egyptian and Beijing campaigns and in the 19th Century, while only 3% of Britain's own budgets were devoted to defence, 25% of colonial India's budget went for the defence of the Empire. British India spent lower than any under developed country's budget on education and public works.

The emperors and sultans before the British used to release grain from their granaries and postponed/reduced taxation during famine years. However, in the case of the Madras famine, Indian grains were exported to the UK, and as a result, millions of locals died—which the rulers attributed to economic theories of Adam Smith etc., in defence of no action by them.

India attained Independence in 1947. Until early 1950s and even thereafter, items such as toothpaste, shoe polish, whiteners (like Blue), floor polish, even processed barley (grain from India taken to Britain, processed and sent back) were all imported. The era then was one of trading and because the British were rulers, naturally British companies were established in India. For example, the trading company called Atlantis (East) in Calcutta was importing products like antiseptics, polishes, and soft drink concentrates. They were the agents for this part of the world and employed other British companies including Parrys, Spencers, Grahams Trading and the like for selling in demarcated parts of India and neighbouring countries.

In the 1950s, the Congress government began with the famous Avadi Resolution on industrial policy and this resulted in many of the foreign companies starting production in India. For example, the Sterling company Atlantis East floated the rupee company called Reckitt & Colman of India. Thereafter, India went for planned development through its Five Year Plans. At some stage, nationalisation of many activities took place. Some foreign companies closed, while others were acquired by Indian interests. For example, Parry and Co, today an Indian company, has diversified into many areas. Muller & Phipps has closed down. Bennett & Coleman, Simpson/Addison group, several textile mills, jute, tea/coffee etc., became Indian. When local manufacture began in the 1950s, it was necessary to "sell" viable quantities of whatever was produced. From trading, we then turned into "selling".

Until the last decade of the last century, we were in what is popularly known as "controlled economy" or "permit-licence raj". The Government—in tune with the changes world over—adopted the concept of free global market economy. This implied our changing ways to become globally competitive and relevant. Thus we entered the age of global relevance, of local actions.

The post-independence economic growth of India is a landmark development. From **swadeshi** concept of Mahatma Gandhi we entered the period of globalisation during 1990s. While Gandhi believed in economic nationalism from village level upwards, Nehru wanted to bring industrial revolution in the country through modern technology. Nehru was partially successful but was impeded in bringing reforms in the economy due to socialist thinking of the then Congress government.

Post-independent India was characterised by low per capita income, low GDP growth, and an economy which kept itself distanced from the capitalist—free trade economy. We had a huge textile industry, large investments in steel manufacturing, a large network of railways, limited automobile production, a host of services like telecommunication, power generation, water supply etc., under the firm grip of government control. It was the believe that the economy should be controlled by government. Banks were nationalised during 1970s. The period is better known as 'licence raj'. Businesses had to procure licences for any and all activities. The bureaucrats controlled the economic activities through series of regulations. Foreign exchange was a rare commodity. This was the period which witnessed rationing of grains, limited choices to consumers in all product categories.

Narasimha Rao and later Rajeev Gandhi opened the doors of the economy for modernisation and globalisation. By mid 1990s the Indian economy had moved to a faster growth rate following the first limited reforms. One example of liberalisation was known as "Broad Banding". In the earlier period if a private sector entrepreneur was given permission to produce something he produced exactly that and nothing else. Broad banding meant that as long as he did not use more raw materials he was entitled to make something else —thus paving way for innovation, that in itself led to an important liberalisation of economy. Another example is that of trucking industry which was deregulated in mid 1980s which meant that people who owned trucks, still in the private sector, were allowed to go out to bid in order to take loads from one part of the country to another at prices they could choose. This was successful in that trucking performance improved and prices were lower as a result of competition instead of going up as predicted by those who had opposed liberalisation. Towards the end of 1980s even though exports were growing rapidly balance of payment pressure were beginning to rise and the budget deficit was increasing. These two things together led to the crisis in 1991 at the time of general election. Despite the debate as to whether there had been liberalisation, 1991 marks the big liberalisation of Indian economy.

Dr. Manmohan Singh as the finance minister introduced a package which swept away controls of the licence raj that brought in gradual liberalisation in investment and trade. The initial moves were to get rid of quantitative trade restrictions. Tariffs were gradually reduced to the point of normal levels, though India is still a fairly protectionist country. Parallely, there was an effort to modernise tax system. In 1991 about one quarter of all tax revenues came out of trade taxes which would be lost with trade liberalisation. Tax rates between one product and another were equalised again gradually over the course of 1990. There was the beginning of divesting the public sector of its ownership of enterprises. India was not adventurous in this respect. It certainly did not do anything like mass privatisation in the former soviet economies. It pursued disinvestment which meant selling minority shares in enterprises on the stock market.

Finally there was financial reform. Where India used to have one stock exchange which still operated pretty much like 19th Century, today it has a modern stock exchange running parallel to that one. The capital issues committee was abolished and companies were allowed to borrow freely. Today, India has rather impressive financial system by developing country standards.

The regional differences between the states within India got sharpened. The fast growing states were in the south and west. The large states of the Gangetic Plains became relatively poorer during the 1990s. Policy which became more attuned to rewarding success has exacerbated these regional differences.

Of late there is a clear indication of dumping philosophy from areas like China, Taiwan, Korea and even Japan. Which country is going to win this race? Most economists think it is good when country grows fast, that it helps another country grow faster. China started with a higher standard of living. It has more manufacturing, a bigger economy, much better infrastructure and a dense network of super highways as against India which is just finishing its first super highway grid linking the four big cities, the ones with more than 10 million people. China also starts off with a high growth rate. It has a high rate of over 40% of GDP of investment. It has practically universal literacy and it has an open economy measuring openness in terms of trade and FDI. India has four major advantages. First, it is into the right things, the modern skill intensive service sectors like IT and BPO. Second it has an entrepreneurial culture. More Indians never fully subscribe to the non-acquisitiveness of the Congress consensus. Now that acquisitiveness has been given free reign, it is producing a big advantage. Third is the fact that they have a much younger population which means that their saving rate is going to increase in the future. A young population with lot of people who are in the high saving phase of their at life cycle is going to save more than an older population as it moves into the retirement phase and may stop active saving. Finally, in many ways India has better institution. It has a tradition of setting up thoughtful committees before it makes a reform. It has a democratic system which is really a major advantage. As countries modernize one of the things people want is a greater say in running their own life. India already has that democracy, China doesn't, and almost every country that's made transition has gone though a pretty traumatic process. May be China will be lucky but India has democratized and does not face the risk. So far the outlook for India is very good.

India, after China, is the second fastest growing economy in the world. In this millennium, there has been a paradigm shift ushering in visible, welcome changes via new policy initiatives, new and fresh visionary approach.

Resurgent India-apart from being number one in several areas-largest producer of dairy products, largest English speaking population, provider of high tech man power to several countries around the world and so on, today is a very attractive and growing centre for foreign direct investment.

The growth is witnessing a boom in the domestic market. Our achievements include a 8 percent economic growth consistently over five years; new breed of qualified young and energetic population; investment in infrastructure be it energy, transportation, roads, ports, education, housing, hospitality and tourism, health care, insurance, agriculture and many more.

Urbanisation is likely to see, by 2025, 37 per cent of Indians accounting for over 60 per cent of consumption, creation of mega cities etc.

We boast being the largest feature film makers in the world. Our growing entertainment world and media industries constitute one of the largest and growing ones.

On the manufacturing and services areas, we have seen all round growth. We passed the 10th million marks in making four wheelers in 2007 and some 5,500 auto component makers. Our exports are on the up. We have low cost/high quality pharmaceutical giants.

Our entrepreneurs are expanding by becoming global. Tatas are in steel production in several countries; Mahindras likewise in tractors. These are but two examples. We are also global in oil exploration and aero space areas.

The emerging challenge for marketers is to plan global/act local.

Summary

Liberalisation, privatisation and globalisation in our country have resulted in a new paradigm for managing the economy. The markets have become borderless and competition demands a new set of skills. Indian companies are showing remarkable agility in managing the markets in this new economy which has thrown open new opportunities and challenges.

Keywords

- Liberalisation
- Privatisation
- Globalisation
- Economic nationalism
- Global economy
- Colonising
- Controlled economy
- Permit licence raj

Discussion Question

1. How are Indian companies managing competition in the new economy?

3

The Marketing Concept

3

The Marketing Concept

Although our subject is Marketing Communications, we need to touch upon Marketing. What is it? In simple terms, it is an exchange of something for either money or for something else. In the case of a product, an organisation has two functions to perform. One is to make the product and the other is to sell this product. It also has to make the product continuously and therefore needs to sell the product continuously. In order for the product to get sold, it should have utility—which can be in terms of when it is needed (called Time Utility). For example, if there is rain, one may need a raincoat or an umbrella; if one is hungry and needs to cook, this person may need oil and the oil producer will need seeds (called Form Utility); consumers will need something like say gas (petrol) to run their vehicles and this needs to be available close to where they live called Place Utility); some consumers may want to own a vehicle (called Ownership utility). So, any product needs to have use or utility for the buyer.

The predecessors to the marketing discipline really began during the first industrial revolution. It all started with barter, very much like the **bandiwala** who exchanges household vessels for used clothing. If the reader has seen early movies made in Hollywood he is sure to have noticed Caucasians exchanging guns and salt for fur and animal skins from Eskimos and other tribals.

The Production Age

During and after the World War I, customers were using the products that the industry could produce and deliver. The quality was confined to the capabilities of the technology available. Due to the limited financial resources and government restrictions the scope to offer variety was limited. The choices to the consumers were limited or even non-existent. For instance, eversince the Land Master design was borrowed from the UK by Hindustan Motors, there was hardly any development in the Ambassador cars from mark I to mark IV in contrast with the currently available models from Hyundai/Maruti Suzuki. Situation was identical in the case of Bajaj Scooters at one point of time when consumers were to wait for an unreasonably long time after making a down payment to get the delivery of the vehicle. This undue delay also created an artificial hike on the extra payment by unscrupulous dealers.

The market has seen dramatic change in scenario soon after policy changes by the government.

Every war has seen technological advances in terms of weaponry and delivery systems. Whatever were the innovations created for war efforts were now adapted for civilian use. Thus, machines that could make machines, aircrafts etc., better ships and faster moving vehicles etc., were some of the many new technological advances that resulted. It is also to be noted that the terrestrial or non-space applications of space technology opening up new vistas for industrialisation. The classic example of the Thermocol and Velchro for domestic consumption is to read an all times record.

The Sales Age

Thereafter, along with the new technology, with more people from the War and otherwise becoming entrepreneurs, more new products came on the market. Some started making competitive products. The earlier production era products as well as the new products were available in larger quantities. They had to be sold. Middlemen/ sales personnel were employed to "sell" the products. They did the selling from their own shops, or sold to other shops or hawked. This was called the Sales era. This lasted until a decade after World War II ended.

The spin off from World War II included new thinking, new knowledge, new technology, etc. Nuclear bombs that wiped out two Japanese cities gave us the technology of nuclear energy. Jet engines have brought larger and faster aircraft. Aerospace and other new sciences like IT and biotechnology have changed our life.

Unlike the earlier periods, post World War II era is also the one when, instead of putting their savings in banks or buying bullion, people have begun investing in shares, thus making possible the formation of mega organisations the world over. Many are in highly competitive fields and as we have said earlier, the market is global, the competition is severe.

The Marketing Concept

The concept of Marketing as opposed to barter, production and sales came into vogue in the 1960s. If one were to look at the earlier Land Labour Capital theory, one would find that without demand for a product, singly or together, these three have no relevance. What would people want? At what price? Where? When? Can products made in another country be sold in different global markets? What would be the tax element in different markets and what are the requirements in each market? In considering all the questions, the fact that the world is getting more educated and vocal has to be taken into account. The result of such education is stringent laws on standards, accountability and so on.

To illustrate the emergence of the marketing concept in an oversimplified way, in1952, James D. Woolf quotes the case of Odo-ro-no. "In the early days of Odo-ro-no, Edna Murphy, daughter of a Cincinnati (USA) surgeon, thought there might be a need for a preparation to stop underarm perspiration and its offensive odour. The formula was her father, Dr. Murphy's, which she compounded in the nights and for a period, sold it house to house during the day. Then she rented a booth (kiosk) on a busy boardwalk of Atlantic City. She extolled the virtues of her product, named Odo-ro-no to passing throngs of astonished females. She had set aside five thousand dollars to advertise her product, but did not spend a cent until she was sure there was a need; it fulfilled the need and people bought and used her product regularly.

James D Woolf also said, "I have the deepest sympathy with the businessman especially if he is operating on a modest capital, who has a new product, different from anything else on the market, and who finds himself unable to decide whether or not he has got something.

"Is there 'bona fide' consumer need for this item? If there is such a need, how universal is it? Is the need as real and so urgent that people will feel justified in the price he has to ask for it?

"This man had exhibited the product to hundreds of his neighbours and his friends, and had circulated some samples, and everybody said 'it is swell.' Why doesn't he put it on the market and get rich? So he takes his problem to a few marketing communications experts —and when he gets through, he is more confused than ever. This businessman and his name is legend, faces an extremely difficult problem. How can he find out, for sure, or almost for sure, that his product will sell repeatedly with advertising without risking too much money?

In the 1950s, the one conclusive way was, to quote Lasker: "FIND OUT WHETHER THE PRODUCT WILL SELL REPEATEDLY WITHOUT ADVERTISING."

Harper describes the marketing concept thus: "The originator of a business usually develops his product from a technical or manufacturing viewpoint and needs to develop sales through effective explanation of his product in terms of consumer wants. To bridge this gap, he makes a product analysis, a detailed study of the product with consumer acceptance as the basis."

We also need to understand changes that take place all the time. For example, the quantum of knowledge has increased from decade to decade, from era to era. We have new fields of knowledge. We have regular census of population and this has now been refined to give us further data such as age, sex, income, occupation and other details. We have studies on lifestyles, called psychographics. We know geography better including the elevation, cold and warm areas, seasons etc. We know where industries are concentrated. We know more about cities and rural areas.

In marketing the more we know the consumer, the better. The study of Psychographics can also be seen as an equivalent of the concept of "culture" as used most commonly in national segmentation.

In the field of buzzwords, marketing, demographics, opinion research, and social research in general, psychographic variables are any attributes relating to personality, values, attitudes, interests, or lifestyles. They are also called IAO variables (Interests, Activities and Opinions). They can be contrasted with demographic variables (such as age and gender), behavioural variables (such as usage rate or loyalty), and firmographic variables (such as industry, seniority and functional area).

Psychographics are often confused with demographics. This confusion can create fundamentally flawed definitions. For example, historical generations are defined by psychographic variables like attitudes, personality formation, and cultural touchstones. The traditionally defined "Baby Boom Generation" has been the subject of much criticism because it uses demographic variables where it should be using psychographic variables. While all other generations are defined by psychographic variables, the old Boomer definition is based on a demographic variable—the fertility rate of its parents.

When a relatively complete profile of a person or group's psychographic make-up is constructed, this is called a psychographic profile. Psychographic profiles are used in market segmentation as well as in advertising.

Some categories of psychographic factors used in market segmentation include: Activity, Interest, Opinion (collectively called AIO).

With more facts to rely on, the marketing concept—when it was accepted and we began using it in practice, fundamental questions that we posed earlier were answered. With modern transportation, it is (as in the case of feature films) possible to release a product all over the world simultaneously. We can find out how and where something could be produced, and work backwards to the product concept itself. It is a step by step and integrated process of determining all aspects of a project/product/concept.

In 1985, the American Marketing Association, rejecting all earlier definitions, described Marketing as:

"Marketing is the process of planning and executing the conception, pricing, promotion and distribution of ideas, goods and services to create exchanges that will satisfy individual and organisational objectives."

In recent times, the need to protect environment and ecology for future generations has given a new dimension to marketing. This is called societal marketing.

Societal Marketing is basically a marketing concept that is of the view that a company must make good marketing decisions after considering consumer wants, the requirements of the company and most of all the long–term interests of the society.

Societal Marketing is actually an offshoot of the concept of Corporate Social Responsibility (CSR) and sustainable development. This concept urges companies to do more than having an exchange relationship with customers, to go beyond delivering products and work for the benefit of the consumers and the society.

Examples

Following are the three examples of Societal Marketing Concept:

1. **Body Shop:** Body Shop is a cosmetic company found by Anita Roddick. The company uses only vegetable based materials for its products. It is also against animal testing, supports community trade, activates self esteem, defend human rights, and overall protection of the planet. Thus it is completely following the concept of Societal Marketing.
2. **Ariel:** Ariel is a detergent manufactured by Procter Gamble. Ariel runs special fund raising campaigns for deprived classes of the world specifically the developing countries. It also contributes part of its profits from every bag sold to the development of the society.
3. **British American Tobacco (BAT):** BAT is a British based Tobacco company. It was found in the year 1902. BAT is involved in working for the society in every part of the world. It conducts tree plantation drives as part of its societal marketing strategy.

In today's competitive environment, there are certain preconditions for the success of a product. These are:

(i) The product must be needed.

(ii) The product must deliver what it promises—it should perform.

(iii) The product must be better than its competitor's.

(iv) The pricing must be right.

(v) The packaging must be viable.

(vi) The positioning must be accurate.

(vii) The brand name must be right.

(viii) The sales force must be very good.

(ix) The trade must be favourable.

(x) The product must be environment friendly.

Summary

Like many developing markets India is evolving from production age to societal marketing concept. The consumer is not only assessing what benefits it gives to the individual but also how it relates to the needs of the society.

Keywords

- Production age
- Sales age
- Societal Marketing
- Sustainable development
- Psychographic

Discussion Question

1. Identify and discuss how some corporate have been successful in societal marketing?

4

Marketing Communications

4

Marketing Communications

Communication indicates sending a message by a sender and, at the other end, receipt of the message by a receiver of that communication followed by a return message process. Marketing communications then is a seller-buyer-seller dialogue, leading to building relationships.

We have mentioned (see chapter 7) the broad functions of the person in–charge of marketing communications in an advertiser's organisation. The brand name, the packaging (and literature) too need to communicate. This person would be involved from that stage.

The promotion mix is related in every conceivable manner to the Product, Brand Name, Packaging, its Price and would include personal communications as also non-personal communications. The task is to get the maximum value for the rupee spent. Thus, the return on investment on marketing communications is what ultimately counts.

In the case of Odo-Ro-No, Ms Edna Murphy did everything: she used personal communications with her target audience—from among the passing crowd, she could choose the kind of ladies she wanted to talk to —show them the product, talk about its virtues, maybe offer a sample or buy back in case dissatisfied, even take the address for follow up and so on. Assuming (a) there was continuous flow of people, (b) it took Edna 10 minutes per contact, (c) she worked for eight hours, she could at best contact a total of 48 persons. She knew she had to reach a much larger numbers of people and had set aside a small budget for advertising.

This example shows us (a) the brand name Odo-Ro-No communicates. We do not have any idea of the packaging

—it could not certainly be the type of under-arm antiperspirant both women and men use today. In Marketing Communications, everything relevant communicates.

Marketing communications can then be said to comprise all activities which would enable the product move from the place of production to the depots, wholesalers, retailers and finally to the actual consumers —again and again and again—infinitum. The same could be said of services offered.

It would be obvious that marketing communications begins even before a product is actually made, that is from its idea or concept stage itself. In the life cycle of a product, marketing communications would play different roles and cover.

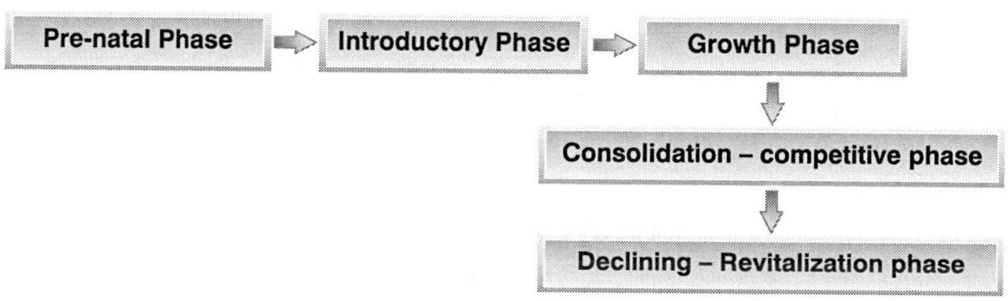

In marketing communications the effort is focused on the consumer. The experts first evaluate this important element in relation to the product. This is done by scanning the data and then testing (as was done for Odo-Ro-No). The Marketing Objectives are then spelt out and emanating out of these, the advertising objectives are laid down. The budget is allocated and then starts the creative and media strategies, the multimedia campaign. The advertising could be pre-tested. Coordinating with other activities, the product and the promotion are launched. All the time, there is a feedback and a system of testing for reactions. Then evaluations take place and this exercise is repeated from one time frame to another.

We shall discuss, in the following chapters, the various communications that are used in marketing. However, these can broadly be categorised into three headings. First is the In-house part, dealing with brand name, packaging, briefs to personnel and the distribution chain. Second is Advertising and Sales Promotion using organised media and the third is Advertising and Sales Promotion using unorganised media. The term unorganised does not denote non-availability but they do not have a fixed rate structure or associations etc., but nevertheless are available—mostly locally.

Marketing Communications work in five ways:

1. Make known/make familiar the Brand name and image of a product or service or idea.
2. Remind people of a temporarily forgotten need.
3. Spread news about new products/ideas/services and create the desire to own, use, adopt, where no desire existed earlier.
4. Urge action through a demonstration of logic and by subtle association.
5. Add subjective value to the objective worth of a product/service/idea.

The Planning of Marketing Communications

Organisations differ in their approach to Planning of Marketing Communications. However, there are two broad approaches practiced in general.

Corporate Approach

Despite changes that take place or even overtake us, there are organisations, which consider promotion as an "extra" cost. Such organisations do believe their product is unique and they are in a good position to dictate terms.

The domestic airlines would be a very good example. There was no alternative to air passengers other than Indian Airlines for domestic flights. The Organisation was not marketing oriented. The rules got changed to suit the Organisation's whims and fancies. For example, most airlines have common-rated rates like, a passenger flying (in either direction) Mumbai-Chennai could pay the same fare for Mumbai-Bangalore-Chennai. This was so with Indian Airlines until one day their management decided to charge sector fares. This was to maximise revenue.

This millennium saw the advent of private airlines. Now, there are all kinds of concessional fares and Indian Airlines (now merged with Air India) is not only marketing oriented but is also innovative in its approach to building relationships.

Another example would be our automotive industry. Before liberalisation, there were just three manufacturers (one went out of business) all in a sellers market—with long wait lists. Similar was the condition with telephones. These were all production oriented.

Marketing-oriented Approach

In organisations that utilise marketing approach, marketing communications is given the importance and seriousness it deserves. Besides, it is notionally treated as a capital expense (reason being APSP—Advertising, Publicity, Sales Promotion as a heading in the Accounting to suit the law in our country, which ensures the entire expense is accounted) and, for every new product, the ROI concept is used. This ROI in some companies, for new products, could be after as much as five years.

In such organisations, outstanding marketing communications is encouraged since this is a source of building competitive advantage, particularly among competing products with little or no difference at all.

Developing Marketing Communications, earlier, involved answering a few questions. These were:

- What are we selling?
- To whom are we selling?
- Where are we selling?
- When are we selling?
- How are we selling?

The answers had to be in great detail—it is not enough to say we are selling a product. We need to describe how it is a better product, the name, competition, etc., and similarly for all the questions.

Since the world of ours is not that simple anymore, we develop marketing communications by going through several steps starting with situation analysis. These steps are:

Selection analysis, review of marketing programme, setting marketing objectives, branding strategy, packaging, positioning strategy, strategic messages, media strategies, promotion strategies, public relations, sponsorship, publicity, sales forces, point of purchase promotion, budget formulation, implementation of communication strategy, and evaluation & feedback.

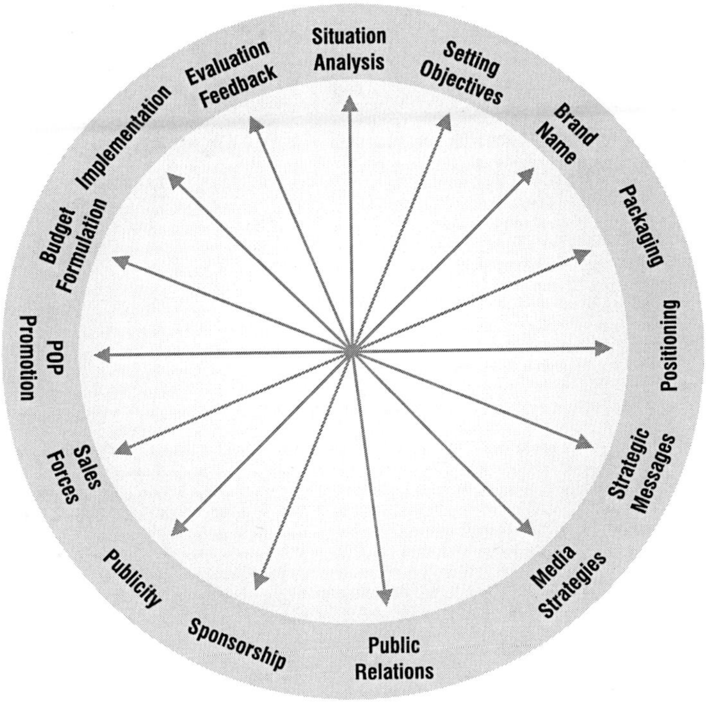

Summary

Marketing communications begin even before a product is actually made. All the elements involved in brand delivery, be it advertising or salesman selling the product, are part of marketing communications. There are two main approaches to the planning of marketing communications. The first one is the corporate approach and the second one is the marketing oriented approach. Corporate approach is company centric whereas the marketing oriented approach is consumer centric. The winning brands take the second route in marketing.

Keywords

- Brand Image
- Prenatal Phase
- Product Life Cycle
- Situation Analysis

Discussion Question

1. Discuss a few brands in the Indian market which are consumer focused.

5

The Communication Process

5

The Communication Process

Communication has been variously defined as transfer of information, ideas, thoughts, between the sender and the receiver. Of course, there must be a purpose to connect the sender and the receiver.

We will be examining the communication process in the context of marketing communication. The communication is a complex process as each element of the process has possibilities which make the process like a network of telephone cables in an exchange.

The source is a brand which must create an identity for it to be recognised by the receiver. The source may or may not be a separate identity to transfer the message. We will examine later how celebrity, testimonials, referral groups, are used as senders to bring credibility to the message. The environments in which the message is delivered and the form in which it is delivered also have implications in influencing the prospects. The visuals, colour, symbols, music, use of emotions can impact perceptions about a brand.

A basic model of communication is given below.

Source/Sender → **Encoding** → **Channel** → **Decoding/Receiver**

The two major participants in the communication process are sender and receiver. The major communication tools are the message and the medium.

The Source: This is the organisation which wants to communicate a sales idea, social thought, information etc., The sender can be simply the organisation, the brand supported by an external agent e.g., a celebrity.

Encoding: Having identified the thoughts to be communicated we must decide how to present it in a form which will influence the receiver favourably. This process of transforming the raw thought is called 'encoding'.

Message: Message needs to be transformed into a form which is understood by the prospect and also must appeal to his cognitive and emotional senses to bring about a change in his behaviour to make a favourable decision in favour of the brand. Here music, visuals, colours, graphics, symbols have a great role to play.

Channel: Having created a message, the marketer identifies a suitable channel through which the message can be transferred to the receiver. Generally decisions requiring rational analysis are more suitable in print media. Products having emotional appeal may fit in broadcast media.

Receiver/Decoding: Decoding is the process of unlocking the message of the sender by the receiver based on his experience, perception etc. The advertiser is successful when the receiver interprets the message as intended.

Noise: The process of delivering a message has to meet the challenges of messages from other advertisers, the programme being watched, and the environment in which the message is being received, the mental condition of the receiver. The external factors contribute to noise or disturbance.

Response/Feedback: The reaction of the receiver is the response which the sender is monitoring. Favourable response is the change on behaviour of the receiver as programmed by the sender.

Based on this feedback the sender may modify his communication strategy.

IMC Planning Process

Integrated marketing communication (IMC) involves coordination of various promotional activities with other marketing activities to effectively communicate with customers. American Association of Advertising Agencies has defined integrated marketing communications as follows :

"A concept of marketing communication planning that recognises the added value of a comprehensive plan that evaluates the strategic role of a variety of communication discipline...for example, general advertising , direct response, sales promotion, and public relations... and combine these disciplines to provide clarity, consistency, and maximum communications impact."

Some researchers have said that the process integrated marketing communication involves the big picture approach to planning and coordination of communication strategy.

IMC ensures a consistent message to the customer through all the components of communication. Integration of various marketing communication messages is important to give a coherent perception of the brand by the customers. IMC helps to prevent duplication and create synergy between various components of communication/ promotion.

IMC gained importance because of the need to manage brands effectively in a competitive market. Brand identity involves logo, symbols, design, packaging and performance of the product. IMC helps in delivering a uniform image of the brand to the customers.

All the components of promotion must be put together and integrated to give a consistent and coherent communication about a brand to consumers.

A model of IMC process is shown below. We will briefly review the various step in IMC process.

IMC Planning Process Model

Review of the marketing plan

Analysis of promotion programme situation

Analysis of communication process

Budget Determination

Develop IMC programme

Integrate and Implement MC strategies

Monitor, Evaluate, Control, IMC programme

Situation Analysis

The first step in developing marketing communications, Situation Analysis, is the very foundation of all other facets of planning. This analysis therefore has to be accurate in every manner. Rigorous upfront assessment of all relevant problems would help in developing the correct marketing communications. This analysis is related to the Marketing Planning that includes market segmentation in all its facets be it geographic, psychographic, benefit or whatever.

In developing marketing communications, the wise person would remember all the time, that right ideas work and not bright ideas.

Right Ideas Work – Not Bright Ideas

The updated databases, market research and facts. The facts alone form the backbone of the situation analysis.

Where Amrutanjan was strongly entrenched in the pain balm market, Vicks found a niche and positioned itself as a Cold Rub. In the toothpaste market, reigned by Colgate, first Promise made a dent with its clove story. Using the same basic story as Colgate's freshness of the mouth, Close-Up used lifestyle (the models used were the younger generation) to bring out freshness of the mouth as opposed to Colgate's authority figure—the dental surgeon.

In depth study, analysis, testing and re-testing of all facts need to go into situation analysis in order to find solutions.

The key factors—both quantitative and qualitative—in situation analysis would relate to:

The Consumer

The Product/Service/Idea

The Competition

The Organisation

The Environment

The Consumer

The consumer is the most important person. Marketing is exchange of his money for the product/service/idea that is offered. Even for industrial products, unless there are consumers for the end product of machinery— e.g., textile machinery used for producing cloth depends on cloth consumption—there will be no demand for machinery if there is no demand for cloth. The better we get to know who our consumer is, the better would be our marketing communications plan.

In situation analysis, we study the consumer as (a) Descriptor, (b) Preceptor and (c) Processor.

(a) Descriptor: This indicates the appropriate (target) audience being studied using various parameters. The three main parameters are Demographics, Geographics, Psychographics and, we name a fourth—Benefit segments.

(b) Perceptor: Indicates sensitivity and understanding and viewing the offer independently .

(c) Processor: Indicates processing information and images the way the communicator intends or even otherwise.

Demographics

Who is the consumer? In terms of age group, sex, education, occupation, marital status, family size etc., and also location, income and other data need to be found out. These details are gathered from the latest census, which incidentally, also gives the difference between the last and latest census.

For example, if for a health product, we are looking at women in the reproductive age group of 15 to 45, in 2001, there were 408.6 million women in this group and the percentage of increase over 2000 was 1.55. We get similar inputs from all sources to complete the profile of the consumer in terms of demography.

By studying further, we can get the trends of say urbanisation, increase in the number of women pursuing higher studies, the type of studies, employment choices and so on.

The latest census and the continuing studies indicate a gender bias in our population. An imbalance has already crept in the ratio of women to men, the former becoming less in number. What would be the implication for society **per se** and thus for marketing and marketing communications? Census and other studies indicate a constant migration of a section of the population and that this is on increase. Do marketing opportunities exist in this market? Questions like these would arise if one were to study data.

If the study were to be of newborns, say for diapers, we need to have data on childbirth and then the income level of the parents etc. Or, if one is making car polish, he will be interested in the number of cars in every town. If it were truck tyres, the manufacturer would be interested in knowing the number of trucks as also the roads they use.

Apart from the census, there are other sources such as the Tata Statistical Outline of India, Marketing Rating Indices by private organisations that give data on the size of key markets, listing them in the order of importance, the Postal pin Code that may be of some use to planners, the Railway stations list and so on, covering most aspects related to demographics. Then there are articles in magazines, year books, answers to questions in the Parliament etc., that also give information.

Psychographics

This aspect of the target consumer is more qualitative in nature. Psychographics deals with "HOW" people live their lives. Research on psychographics costs a lot. People under observation act differently and tend to exaggerate. Therefore, for reliability, the questions asked would try and separate facts from life, the sample size would be fairly large and various methods (interviews, direct mail, phone etc.,) would be used to cross verify the results. Since the study endeavours to understand the "psyche" and attitude of the target group, the questions asked would be around 300 or more and some of these would be on the lines of:

- I do not take chances at all.
- I like fast cars.
- A woman should not wear jeans.
- I watch only the news on the TV.
- It is important people wash their hands before and after every meal.
- I like classical music.
- I love parties where I meet lots of interesting people, find gaiety and listen to gossip.
- I like trekking.
- I am working to become a big shot and my goal is to achieve this in about five years if not less.

Psychographic studies are undertaken for individual product groups since attitudes would differ, for example, cleanliness vs adventure. These studies are also related to two kinds of variables: enduring and/or dynamic.

Psychographic studies reveal Dynamic variables, specifically the relationship between a product group and the consumer and also knowledge of the products desired and/or derived benefits, quantity of usage, frequency of usage, and so on.

Enduring variables relate to demography, geography and in recent times, in particular in the IT industry, this aspect also plays a part in revealing more about the people on the move or constantly travelling.

In marketing communications planning, dynamic variables help in "Positioning" (about which we will study later) and in creating the communications, while enduring values help in media strategy and planning.

Some aspects of psychography are included in the data made available by media—who have used research and tell us about their audience in terms of ownership of items like vehicles, washing machines, holiday travel, banking, insurance and other inputs. These are, however, in general terms and not so specific. What we really need to know is the brand they use, when they would replace, how they would finance their purchase, what factors influence choice of a particular brand, the impact of festivals on purchases etc.

Another aspect of lifestyle studies can be seen in a few people owning their own aircraft or using luxury cars—which could be associated with their status/ego/wanting to be different. Among Indian women, it is the type of jewellery they wear. This is called custom-oriented exclusive segment.

Geographics

This aspect helps the planner understand and discriminate between urban, sub-urban, rural, etc., locations and also the climate, elevation, communication facilities such as roads to begin with, and other factors related to his topic. Geographically the country can be divided as Eastern India/Western India/ Northern India and Southern India. Or it can be divided into states and in each state into towns, districts, even wards; or into pin code area. Then, using the market rating indices, the places can be listed in the order of priority. For agricultural products, geographical information would also indicate the types of crops, seasonality etc. Or, for hill stations, the tourist seasons.

Benefit: There is a group of people who look for benefits at least risk. For example, lottery or other means of making a quick buck.

There are several other aspects of the consumer, which need to be studied in the situation analysis.

Usage Level/End Use

For any product, there are heavy and light users. For example, take ties or suits that men wear. There are people who wear these every day and also change the attire for morning and evening and for partying. There are others who wear them only occasionally. Or take expensive Banaras sarees, which are used by most only on special occasions. For a product, first we need to know all users, then the heavy and light users.

What is the end use? Take cooking oil as an example. There are people who use what is popularly known as **desi ghee** in food and for frying. They do not mind being fat. On the other hand, there are people who are figure conscious and they use non-saturated oils and avoid frying because they want to stay slim. Some people buy things like a painting as a hobby while for some it is either asset formation or they are dealing in that article.

Take a product like razor blade. It could be for shaving and, for school children, it could be for sharpening pencils. Or take incense sticks: They could be for prayer or just for fragrance. There will always be a heavy end use and an alternative, lighter use for most products.

If we have the information why people buy a product and how much they use it, this information helps in segmenting the users as heavy and light and in determining how to reach them.

Time of Adoption

When does one accept and adopt a product? Normally early adopters tend to be the young generation, because they are more adventurous, cosmopolitan, more educated, have higher income and social mobility as against late adopters. New products such as diapers in our country are adopted and used by those who are in a higher income level and for the newborn until it is potty trained. On the other hand, it is only the older people who think of life insurance/ medical insurance/a roof above their head and such matters. While the young think of holidays in beach resorts and hill stations, the elders think of religious places and pilgrimages.

Information Source

The source of information would be interpersonal, the media, the Internet, peers, the library, published data and more. The information sought would depend on the problem. For a person getting married and setting up his/her own household, that person seeks information on housing, medical attention, schooling, domestic help and so on.

For the first time pregnancy, information is sought from the doctors and books.

Brand Loyalty Factor

A relationship between the user and the brand used is built systematically over several years. Consumers buy "satisfaction" and not products. They do not wish to risk their hard earned money on new or unknown or suspect brands, even if they are better. Their faith is such they are unlikely to switch to another brand.

On the other hand, there are people who buy any brand.

The consuming public can, in actual practice, be divided into three groups:

Group 1: Totally Loyal: This group will not, under any circumstances, use a different brand. If they are heavy users, it is enough to keep the brand name in their minds by reminders at calculated intervals. The light users need to be persuaded to use more through logical means.

Group 2: Switchers: This group will try anything and for various reasons. Such reasons can include attractive name, the package or the price or he sees the product and wants to try it himself. To woo them will take intense and sustained effort.

Group 3: Loyal to competition: This group is fiercely loyal to a competitive brand. No amount of effort is likely to win them to our brand. These customers over a period of time find total satisfaction in the competitor brand and therefore will not see any reason for brand switching.

Need and Benefit

The customer needs to be studied by asking these questions: Why do they need this product? What are the benefits they think this yields them? In this context, Haley Russel (Journal of Marketing, July 68) has segmented benefits of toothpaste as an example:

The benefits observed were Flavour, Appearance of the product, Brightness of teeth, Decay-prevention and Price.

The users were classified as four segments: Sensory, Sociable, Worrier, Independent. Russel related these segments to demographics, psychographics etc., in order to illustrate that the same manufacturer could cater to all the segments but with different brands and appeals:

Segments	Sensory	Sociable	Worrier	Independent
Principal Benefitsought	flavour product	Brightness appearance	Decayofteeth	Price
Demographics	Children	Teenagers Young	Large family	Men*
Brands dis-proportionately favoured	Colgate Stripe	McLean Ultrabrite	Crest	Any brand
Personality Traits	High self-involvement	High sociability	Hypochondriac	High autonomy
Lifestyle	Hedonistic	Active	Conservative	Valueoriented

Since then the scene has changed and America today is an equal opportunity employer and women too need to be included in this category.

Hierarchy of Effect

Haley Russell's thesis on segmentation also reveals that, consumer grouping, awareness, attitude, interest, etc., of consumers all interact and shift when the message

- stresses a benefit
- is shown to the right audience

CAPP

John Maloney, taking note of the benefit segmentation hierarchy of effect, etc., developed the CAPP or Continuous Advertising Planning Programme. He used several parameters and two hypothetical situations:

Parameters	Situation One	Situation Two
Presenceinmarketplace	100%	100%
Awarenessintargetgroup	80%	80%
Attitude prior to use	10%	70%
Trial purchase	8%	60%
Repeat purchase	6%	6%

Situation One reveals that marketing communications has created "awareness" and nothing more. Situation Two reveals that awareness and the attitude towards purchase followed by trial purchase were both high. When we look at repeat purchase, both situations show the same figure. The reasons for the fall in percentage from trial to repeat in situation Two could be due to reasons such as overselling or claims in advertising that did not prove to be true.

The CAPP model has been mentioned in order to stress the importance of continuous monitoring of advertising and also continuously understanding the shifts in the parameters.

Kotler too, in his book **Marketing Management,** advocates continuous watch and suggests four common strategies:

- Undifferentiated
- Wholly differentiated
- Concentrated
- Partially differentiated

Media strategies: Shotgun or the Rifle shot approach, depending on the product/budget/strategy and other aspects.

These strategies are further discussed under MEDIA.

Reference and Peer Group

When a consumer is interested in a new product (usually expensive) or is in a new situation in life e.g., the young couple expecting their first child, he or she looks to other experienced people for guidance and advice. Reference group consists of people who have experience which is taken as authentic and consumer adopts it. Peer group refers to people of the same rank in the workplace or similar age in the society who are also experiencing similar situations and therefore the consumer copies the behaviour without hesitation.

Since the purpose of undertaking situation analysis is to get to know the consumer as thoroughly as possible, there are many other aspects of study too.

The Consumer Life Cycle

How does a consumer process information and over a period of time, how does he behave?

John A. Howard, author of **Consumer Behaviour—Application of Theory,** shows us that, for any product the consumer goes through a series of stages of information processing and decision making. Howard calls these:

1. Extended Problem Solving or EPS
2. Limited Problem Solving or LPS
3. Routinised Response Behaviour or RRB

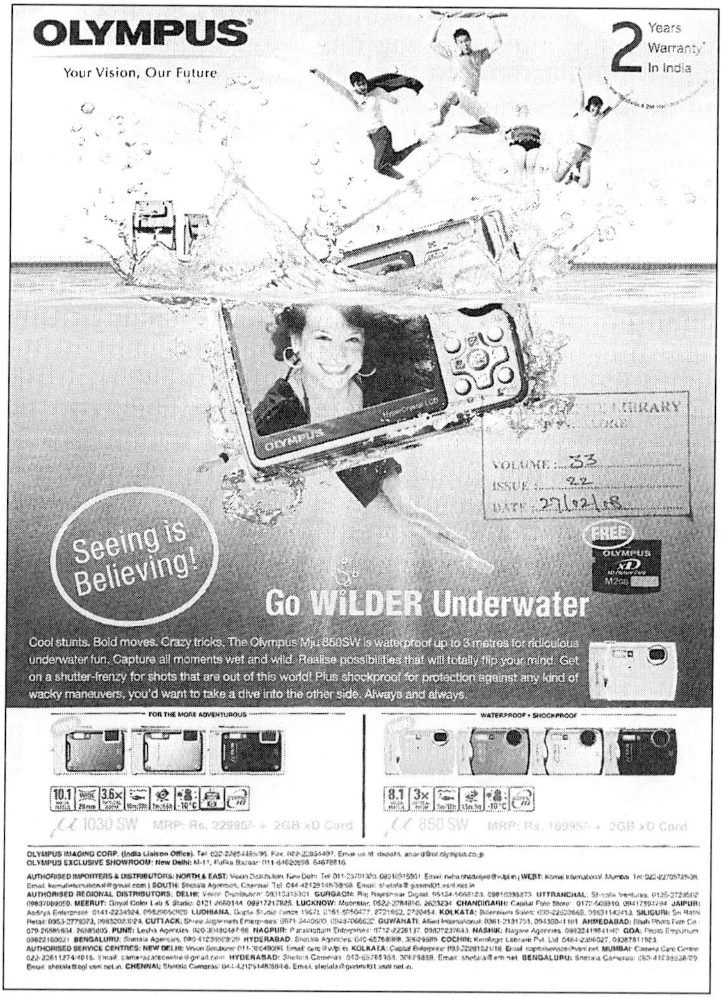

Fig. 5.1: Advertisement for underwater camera—an example of Extended Problem Solving (EPS)

For a first time use of a product, the consumer, who has no knowledge of this, would go to great lengths to learn. As an example, take a farmer who wishes to change from say sugar cane to oil seeds. He would take all the time needed to learn about growing oil seeds, the cost and benefits, season, yields, inputs etc. He would visit other farmers who have succeeded with oil seeds, talk to the agricultural specialists etc. and then only change. The processing of information takes a long time and he solves his problem through Extended Problem Solving (EPS).

The same farmer, when the crop is growing faces a pest problem. He gets answers pretty fast from his usual sources. This is Limited Problem Solving(LPS).

Assume he keeps on cultivating oil seeds for a few years. He becomes an expert and whatever problem arises, he routinely solves these and this is his behaviour routinised response behaviour (RRB).

In marketing communications, when a product is launched, it is necessary to give a lot of information and take the consumer through the EPS way. When the product is established and people know about it, the advertising gives less information but visually reinforces its position. Thereafter it is a question of reminder—RRB —advertising to the existing audience and other efforts towards new audience.

As an example, let us take moulded luggage in India. This was a new concept and the material used was light. Indians, accustomed to steel trunks, wooden boxes and leather cases, needed to be educated on the toughness of the luggage. The appeal was toughness together with style. (Television advertising demonstrated the toughness through a railway porter handling heavy pieces. Style advertising showed carry-with-you luggage for frequent flyers.)

Then the luggage was promoted as part of lifestyle, with flyers and car owners as main users. Thereafter, it is less of advertising and more of reminders. Moulded luggage promotion has taken the audience through all the three stages.

From the viewpoint of marketing, therefore, when a new concept or product is launched, a lot of information needs to be given. When the demand grows, less information would suffice and once the product gets established, routine reminder advertising would be adequate.

This can be illustrated as follows:

		Scale	
	0	5	10
Introduction	EPS	LPS	RRB
Growth	LPS	RRB	EPS
Maturity	RRB	EPS	LPS

Yet another author, Rogers, suggests that since each stage requires different information processing, each requires creative approaches (innovation) to match the processing style. He calls these

1. Discontinuous Innovation
2. Dynamically continuous Innovation
3. Continuous Innovation

Another expert, Howard, describes these three stages as Concept Formation, Concept Attainment and Concept Achievement.

Howard describes characteristics of the Consumer Life Cycle vis-à-vis EPS, LPS and RRB as follows:

Consumer		Stage	
	EPS	LPS	RRB
Relevantinformationin long-term memory	Little	Moderate	Lots
Amountofinformation needed	Lots	Moderate	Little
Speed of decision	Slow	Moderate	Mixed
Focus of search	External	Mixed	Internal
Conceptdevelopment	Information	Attainment	Achievement/Utilisation

Thus in EPS, the consumer is unfamiliar with a new product/problem or its concept. He needs lots of information. He evaluates the information and is very cautious. He takes, naturally, plenty of time to arrive at a decision. Since he himself is not an expert, he seeks external sources for explanations he needs. In LPS, all these change and in RRB, the changes are much more.

From the studies done by both Rogers and Howard, it will be evident that a marketing communicator would do well to continuously assess how much and what type of information needs to be provided to the consumers.

Consumer Involvement

Do consumers care very much about brand choice decision when buying a product? The level of caring or motivation is described as the level of involvement (and today also as Brand Equity or Brand Franchise or Relationship Ratio). The level is important in developing marketing/marketing communications strategies.

What is involvement? This has been defined by Freedman as "Commitment to a position or concern with a specific stand on an issue," and by Festinger as "Concern with the issue itself."

We need to relate consumer involvement with products. Generically described, almost all consumers use toothpaste, shaving blades, incense sticks, soaps, etc. When it comes to specific brands, involvement of consumers with brands differs. Normally, there is low involvement with frequently bought consumer goods—where many brands appear similar and there is little perceived difference and therefore there is little risk.

Brand franchise/share of the market is built by getting the consumer involved—in one or a multiplicity of ways such as style, uniqueness (like clove in a toothpaste), efficiency, price, past experience and so on.

A highly motivated consumer has a positive attitude towards a particular brand. Although normally such degree of involvement is seen in consumer durables, this is also increasingly evident in consumables such as a shaving blade, soap, deodorant and so on. To such a consumer the choices offered are not similar. On the other hand, a consumer who is not typically motivated would be happy to take any of the acceptable brands since the manufacturers of these are reputable or for any other reason.

The marketing communicator would have to properly plan his communication mix and not depend only on advertising and sales promotion. The possible strategies, which need of course to be tested for individual problems, for highly involved and less involved consumers are as follows:

Type I	Type II
(Highly involved)	**(Less involved)**
Awareness Advertising Primarily print media High information Low frequency (repetition) Longer messages (copy) Broadcastforbasicawareness	**Awareness** Advertising Primarily broadcast Low information Highfrequencyrepetition Shorter messages Uniquesellingproposition
Attitude Personal selling Trial Demonstration Promotiontobringconsumer To retailer	**Behaviour** Advertising Promotion/Induce trial Pricing, Promotion Packaging
Behaviour Product Price Pricing Promotions	**Attitude** Product Usage
Long-run behaviour Product Warranty Service Promotions	**Long-run behaviour** Advertising Product Pricing

The relationship between the product and the consumer is such that —for example among vehicle users, it will be seen that a station wagon is found to evoke less emotion than a sports car—attitudes differ for even the same product group.

For the marketing communicator, it is important to understand the subtle differences and realise that awareness creating advertisements would differ from attitudinal creation advertisements. Emotion, rationality etc., lead to differences in thinking, feeling and response, both among High Involvement and Low Involvement categories.

One other author, Henry Assael studied the two types of consumers in 1984 and has offered the following chart:

High Involvement Active Established Consumer	Low involvement Passive (Newer) consumer
Consumers	**Consumers**
Are source of information	learn information randomly
Seek information	gather information
Represent an active audience for Communication	represent a passive audience for marketing Communications.
Effectivecommunicationonthemis strong	Effective communication is weak.
Evaluate brands before buying	Buyfirst,evaluation ifdoneislater
Seekmaximumexpectedsatisfaction So,comparebrands,assessbenefits on several attributes	Seek some acceptable level of satisfaction, and buy a brand least likely to give problem. Buying decisionbasedonfewerattributes Familiarity is the key here
Personality/Lifestylecharacteristic relatedtobehavioursinceproductis tiedcloselytoconsumers'identity/ belief systems	Personality/lifestylecharacteristics notrelatedtoconsumers'identityor belief system.
Reference group influences in large measure Because of product importance to group norms and values	Referencegroupsexertlittleproducts unlikelytoberelatedtoGroupnorms and values.

At an international advertising conference, Richard Vaughn of Foote Cone Belding Communications (a leading advertising agency) took a look at "involvement" models in terms of and tabulated them as follows:

THINK	FEEL	DO	REACT

THINK–High Involvement–relates to new products and items like car, house and furniture i.e., High value.

Model of involvement would be learn, feel, do and in doing so, economic factors too play a part.

Implication for the marketing communicator would be to test recall, analyse results.

Media strategy for the communicator would be long copy, reflective vehicles.

Creative would be specific, informative, demonstrative.

FEEL–High involvement–effective: relates to product such as jewellry, perfumes, fashion apparel etc.
Model would be Feel-Learn-Do – Lifestyle/Psychographics.
Implication: Change Attitudes, arouse emotion.
Media: Use large space/longer duration broadcast to create usage. Use special vehicles.

DO–Low involvement/ Habit formation. Items such as food, household goods etc.
Model – Do – Learn – Feel
Implication – Test sales
Media: Smaller advertisements, television and radio broadcasts
Creative: Reminder

REACT – Self Satisfied. Items including cigars/biscuits/soaps
Model – Test sales
Media: Point of purchase, outdoor, print
Creative: Attention getting

According to Vaughn, this is not a formula but a thought-starter, to ponder, study and think of the right answers to the situation and problem. In fact all situations he illustrated do not fall into any of the four models and the marketing communicator would therefore do well to undertake relevant study to find out the right answers.

While sifting all data relating to the consumer, often it would be difficult to distinguish between a problem and an opportunity, because every problem creates an opportunity or vice versa.

Expertise and confidence levels would develop in the marketing communicator only with hands on repeated exposure to work situations, problems and opportunities.

The Product/Service/Idea

An organisation decides on a product or service or an idea after considerable study and at some risk. If it is a pharmaceutical product, it will need tests, clearances and studies. If it is an engineering product, to perform and be better than other products in the market. We mentioned earlier that Vicks pitched itself as a Cold Rub and not as a pain reliever. And Promise toothpaste played up the clove content to distinguish it from other toothpastes (when all toothpastes do contain clove oil).

We need to recall the preconditions for successful marketing communications:

The product must be (i) needed, (ii) must deliver, (iii) must be better, (iv) must be right for the chosen audience, (v) packaging must be viable, (vi) pricing should be right, (vii) positioning should be accurate and on target, (viii) brand Name must be correct, (ix) trade and distribution network should be favorable, (x) environmentally friendly.

Organisations look at trends and the reason why the product exists in their production mix. They also ask questions such as "what is the life cycle stage of this product? Whatever they do is continuously assessed and backed by a Research and Development Department.

Competition

The very first competition is for the consumers' money. Therefore the product/service/idea that the company offers should enjoy sufficient priority. The next area of competition is new innovations. For example, electric grinder replaced the traditional stone very fast. A washing machine replaced domestic help. Existing habits and attitudes can change as it is happening with packaged branded spices used by housewives, replacing the traditional home ground ones.

A product competes with other products in the market. Nirma took away a considerable share of the market enjoyed by well-entrenched brands. The strategy used by Nirma was to highlight the lower price of Nirma compared to others. Some manufacturers manage competition by buying out competing brands and gradually withdrawing them subsequently. A few years back Hindustan Lever bought out Tata brands and over a period of time some of the Tata brands became extinct from market shelves. Yet another strategy adopted by some manufacturers is to extend the brands of the same product to cover additional utility and prevent entry of new competitors. For example, Colgate, Colgate salt, Colgate fluoride, Colgate fresh. When markets were threatened by health risks connected with certain products the manufacturer resorted to modifying the product to remove the fear of risks associated with the product. Example, Suffola oil with low fat content. Some manufacturers used even unethical practices to compete. A blade manufacturer had actually taken competititor's stocks out of dealers shelves, dipped them in water until rust was noticed, repacked and placed them back on dealers, shelves.

Another manufacturer, even to this day, spreads the rumour that using a particular brand of domestic detergent is harmful for hand.

A marketing communicator needs to study all forms of competition, trends and also how strong is the established competition. He or she also needs to study the nature of competition, which may be cut-throat, gentlemanly or something else. In short, a SWOT analysis needs to be made of each and every competitor. The character of competition has a bearing on the nature and content of marketing communications.

The Organisation

Organisations could be one-man, a partnership, a cottage industry, a small-scale industry, a proprietary one, a joint stock company, a not for profit one, a cooperative, a public sector undertaking, a franchisee, an importing agency, a representative office in India or as branches in India and so on. An organisation can be local, regional, national or international. It could be an industrial concern, an agricultural body or a consumer company in the areas of durables, perishables, services etc.

In the marketplace, an organisation is associated with some or the other human reference term. We tend to call a company as blue chip or conservative, dependable and so on. Our concern here is marketing communications and it is from this viewpoint that we need to look at the following facets of the organisation:

1. Is the organisation designed to serve the needs and wants of chosen markets?
2. Is marketing planning developed to serve different market segments/countries?
3. Is planning complete in that the marketing system takes into account every facet—suppliers, distribution channels, transportation, competition, customers, environment and more?
4. How well is the marketing department integrated and controlled within the organisation?
5. How well organised is new product development?
6. How well organised is continuous upgradation of existing product lines and Research and Development?
7. How is marketing information organised?

8. How does the organisation adapt itself to change?
9. How efficient is the organisation/its manpower?
10. How well are the marketing resources used?
11. What is the philosophy of the organisation on sharing information with creators of advertising?

The eleventh question needs to be enlarged. There are many organisations which treat information confidential and do not share even vital statistics with their advertising agency. A good marketing communicator would treat (and even have this aspect written down as a condition in the contract with the agency) the advertising agency as a partner in marketing. He would confide every piece of relevant and irrelevant information with the agency. He would brief the agency on the outlook for the product group as a whole, for his brands, major reasons behind sales performance in the past, competitive information, product strengths/weaknesses, segmentation details, user profiles, the distribution mechanism, past promotion, budgets etc.

The Environment

The environment is made up of the state of the nation, its economy, Gross National Product, Gross Domestic Product. The per capita income and expenditure patterns, the shifts and shares of different employers and new outlook thereof, Government's policies at the Union and States levels, plans, taxation and other control mechanisms, competition, the change in lifestyle of the people. Market intelligence throws up sudden unexpected opportunities—when coffee crop failed in Brazil, India had a bonanza; in 1991, when the chilli crop failed in China, Indian exporters did very well; in 2005, because of unprecedented floods in India, the country imported onions from Pakistan. We need to know media shifts, cost escalations and the like and also keep a watch on the anciliary services used.

From the marketing communication point of view we need to as well like Right to Information, Consumer Acts etc., as well as ethics.

Conclusion

The situation analysis aims at getting together every single fact and information about the consumer and related aspects and is perhaps the most important exercise the marketing communicator needs to undertake. Since the world itself changes, it is equally important to update the data often, sometimes the same day! All facts and figures need to be double checked.

Summary

Communication process involves a source/sender, encoding of the message, the media/channel to be used, decoding/understanding by the prospect. Finally there has to be a response in the form of purchase of a product/service.

Integrated marketing communication planning process involves review of marketing plan, analysis of the promotion programme situation, analysis of communication process, budget determination, development of IMC programme, integration and implementation of marketing strategies. Finally monitor, evaluate and control the integrated marketing communication programme.

Keywords

- Communication Process
- High Involvement
- Continuous Advertisement
- Consumer Life Cycle
- Peer Group
- Brand Loyalty Factor
- Low Involvement
- Planning Programme
- Reference Group

Discussion Question

1. Discuss involvement theory in planning communication strategy.

6

Advertising Purpose and Benefits

6

Advertising Purpose and Benefits

What has promotion achieved?

There is a debate as to the role of advertising in marketing of products. Many are of the view that advertising leads to increase in the cost of the product. Some opine that advertising creates wants for products which are not necessary. Advertising is also criticised for exploiting emotional weakness of women and children. However, the truth of usefulness of advertising lies in understanding the economic role it plays in promoting the business. Major contributions to the business and society are discussed here.

(i) Advertising leads to

(a) better merchandise

(b) lower prices

Advertising makes it possible for the consumer to spread his purchasing power over more merchandise, thus creating still greater demand for other advertised products. Ours is a mass-production era and manufacturing plants, large or small, are able to pass savings by large-scale or planned production to their customers. At the same time, they maintain viable profits. Inflation and/or taxes have not changed this basic value. If anything, they place more pressure on producers to achieve still greater efficiency by mass production. We do not buy generic products anymore: we choose trust and quality, which is better than taking risk of unknown generic products and therefore buy brands.

Mass production puts within the reach of the average consumer all types of household, personal, office and factory conveniences. It makes available such taken for granted things as light bulbs and such new wonders as a laptop/cell phone. As more and more brands compete, the price factor is also an area of competition and we get the benefit of lower prices.

(ii) Advertising helps cut the cost of distribution

Advertising makes possible for the manufacturer to contact more distributors, dealers, consumers and more production managers, purchasing agents, plant foremen—in more places, more quickly and to secure quicker action than any other method of communication he can use.

The value of a force like advertising cannot be judged on the basis of its cost, but rather in its cost-result ratio. How much would it cost to contact one person by post? Rs.5 as postage alone. On the other hand, a newspaper reaching lakhs of readers would cost us a few rupees per thousand readers—called the 'mille rate' or 'cost per thousand readers per unit of advertising'. For example, the cost of a full page in one of India's largest circulated weeklies, Kumudam, works out to 300+ readers per rupee! Per contact, it is a fraction of a paise. Thousands of viewers pass a hoarding. The cost per head would be a fraction of one paisa. Media compete with one another in offering cost effective reach.

Advertising may not be a match to personal selling. However, by making the product known and desired, it makes selling that much easier. It certainly carries information to the distribution network in addition to making the consumer aware of the product in a favourable manner.

(iii) Advertising offers choice

When a product succeeds in the market, competitive products by other manufacturers appear, some with improvements and the consumer—in a short period—is offered a variety to choose from. There are also alternative choice : for example, in food, one can today choose types of cuisine, such as Italian, Japanese, Mexican and others—unknown in the local market a few years ago.

(iv) Advertising helps to better products, new products, innovation

During the last few decades, new conveniences that have appeared in the market include the radio, later on the transistor radio, electric or gas cooking range, electric iron, hand-wound, automatic and thereafter quartz wrist watches, the television (including the latest flat ones, the cellphone, laptop computers, mopeds, even conveniences like laminations, and many more. Similarly, we have witnessed (and continue to do so) innovations in the areas of health care. In the workplace, we have automation, robotics and more. Without advertising that creates greater spending and profits, there would have been less job creations, and investment on what is popularly known as 'research and development' or 'innovations'.

(v) Advertising is the vehicle through which our industrial know-how is spread and augmented

Industrial advertising is performing the vital task of channeling know-how into the plants where it is needed in order to maintain and improve efficiency of our big and small industries.

(vi) Advertising helps set up the channels of physical distribution and keep them streamlined

The normal movement of merchandise from manufacturer to the distributor, then from distributor to retailer (and thereafter the consumer) is propelled all the way by advertising. Advertising tells the trade the facts about the goods, helps them decide which items will sell best in their operating area, shows them how to get the most value out of the consumer advertising done for respective brands.

It also is the means of selling equipment for modern retailing to the trade—inducing more retailers all the time to tool up for modern merchandising, streamlined materials handling, and greater efficiency.

Marketing know-how is passed down the line through the advertisements in merchandising papers, e-mail, direct-mailing, audio visuals, presentation books and all other means of trade communication. And the manufacturer—contacting the trade in all parts of the country and beyond—also serves as a clearing-house of information, passing the good ideas of one retailer to others through the appropriate channels of communication.

(vii) Advertising speeds up the introduction of new products that are needed

Advertising quickens the acceptance of new items and creates such acceptance at least cost.

The new but small Advertiser usually starts in one limited market, thence expands market after market, reinvesting first profits in an unusually large amount on promotion until national distribution finally is reached.

The established Advertiser, on the other hand, is more apt to utilise the national acceptance of his already known merchandise to carry new items into the distribution in all parts of the country at the same time. He would very likely have run tests in representative markets on his new product first. He can also test his advertising before going national.

(viii) Advertising safeguards the position of established products for which there is still a need

With the market constantly bombarded by new products and new versions of old products, the Advertiser must keep vigil to safeguard his market position. The fact that his merchandise still fulfils a need is not enough. He has to keep reminding people the benefits his product continues to offer. By doing so, the advertiser thwarts the attempts of rivals to steal customers away. He also safeguards against other types of merchandise which sap consumer of his purchasing power.

(ix) Advertising enables the manufacturer of products that are becoming obsolescent, to switch to new products

When obsolescence is certain, an established advertiser can switch more quickly and more surely to new products that fulfil a need.

An example is the courier services in our country that forced the Postal Department (discontinue Express Delivery and to introduce Speed Post and thereafter many customer-friendly offers.

(x) Advertising is a competitive weapon for both the new comer and the established concern

It is democratic to have open competition for the consumer's money. Advertising helps keep competition open where the discerning consumers know who is making what, how much it costs, where it is available for purchase, why manufacturers believe their product offers a bigger benefit than the competition.

The newcomer has as good an opportunity as the established manufacturer to sell his products. The result is a free competitive market and more choice. The public gets a full view of what the choice is in products, quality and prices. The product which gives consistent value, fulfills consumer needs , has styling and quality wins-aided to a large degree by the quantity and character of the advertising that exposes it.

Advertising is also in itself exposed and the advertising that is in better taste, more informative, more in line with the way potential consumers want to be informed succeeds.

(xi) Advertising protects against destructive price competition

While advertising in general tends to reduce prices, there are situations of price wars—where competition resorts directly to reduced price, indirectly by offering more quantity for the same price, bribes in the form of free gifts etc. This situation threatens quality and stability of future production because price is the only consideration for sales. Advertising—holding the price line, telling the consumers why as well as stressing quality at a fair price—can and does safeguard a brand and its relationship with the consumers. Although there may be a temporary drop in sales it is quality and fair price that help win the situation.

(xii) Advertising helps stabilise a business

By its very nature, advertising looks to the future as well as at the present. It builds market acceptance in advance, and leads to stable operations.

It stimulates sales activity when any part of the market tends to slow down and eliminates seasonal slumps. Off-season promotion results in the creation of what amounts to new marketing seasons in many fields. An impressive example of this is the fans and refrigerator markets.

(xiii) Advertising smokes out new prospects

Advertising aims at a specific audience called the target consumers. However, because of advertising, quite often, more customers surface—people the manufacturer might never have thought of as prospects. In this context, while market research may determine where most of the sales potential for a product exist, it cannot locate all the usual sources of sales.

When used as a prospect locater, advertising may in itself be a tool of market research.

(xiv) Advertising keeps them sold

Advertising reassures the new owner that he has made a wise purchase. The new owner, usually alert to advertising of the product he has just bought, is given no chance to doubt its value. He keeps reading and hearing (or seeing) about the quality of his new possession. He becomes not only a happy customer but also a booster of the product, since the best advertising is a satisfied customer.

(xv) Advertising is a key sales tool for the sales person:

The sales person calling on dealers, in the case of industrial products on organisations, for pharmaceutical products on doctors, for office products on business organisations or for certain household appliances on the housewife, gets a valuable identity because advertising has already made these people aware of the product/ company behind it.

(xvi) Advertising covers marginal sales territories, releases salesmen for selective selling

Selling costs tend to rise but the price does not go up because of competition and the theory that the higher the price the lower the sales and vice versa. The selling organisation needs to control the selling costs. Resorting to cost-return analysis, selling organisations skip low volume outlets or even whole territories because of low demand, transportation costs and such aspects. Retail volume is becoming concentrated to an ever greater extent in fewer marketing areas, fewer retail outlets. Sales personnel have to concentrate on areas which have sales potential. Advertising is used to contact consumers in the marginal territories and outlets at less cost. Alternative marketing exercises—a local wholesaler, a part time agent, direct order etc., take the role of the sales personnel (and in the absence of personal contact, the attention given to these territories will not yield the same results.)

(xvii) Advertising reaches people who cannot be reached normally/or who would not see a sales person

Many doors, such as the chairman's in an organisation, are closed to sales personnel. However, advertising in the media makes known the product/service/idea even to such people.

(xviii) Advertising helps procure the best in materials and manpower

Success of any good organisation also depends on securing the very best materials and man-power at fair prices. Well-known companies are contacted first by the suppliers of raw materials and the job seeker. The company, in turn, has the power to choose the very best and thus stay ahead in the field.

(xix) Advertising establishes friendly relations with the public

The public relations aspects of advertising are given increasingly serious attention than ever in the past. Done well, this leads to what is today called 'relationship building' and 'relationship marketing', where the consumer himself becomes the advocate for the company/ brand.

(xx) Advertising increases the capital value of a business

Advertising is a factor in profits both because it can reduce selling costs and also it contributes to more and faster sales volumes. Advertising builds the company and its services/branded products. It is a real investment in building the names as assets—a fact realised by the investing/financing fraternity. Companies that advertise consistently and are known to have a stable/growing business find it easier than non-advertisers to borrow at low rates for business expansion, plant improvement and more. Some would pay royalties to use just a brand name for their product (e.g., a famous garment name for a wrist watch or a liquor brand for a lighter). This in turn enhances share values and the name itself has great financial value and therefore a great asset. The stocks of companies which advertise are the most valuable.

(xxi) Advertising protects consumers against infringers

A registered trademark is the property of its owners and advertising proves its existence as also value as far as the law is concerned. There are unscrupulous people who imitate the trademark of well-established brands and pass this on as the original. One of the most helpful pieces of evidence in any court of law is the proof of advertising portraying the trademark. All manufacturers keep a vigil against imitation and infringement in order to protect their relationship with their customers as trusted organisations.

(xxii) Advertising is a public service – used in public interest

The government departments advertise to inform the concerned public. Examples include the payment of tax/public hearings on key matters/appeals when disaster strikes—for blood and other kinds of donations. In addition, during recent times, many NGOs have emerged to tackle specific tasks. Their efforts are supported by advertising (also called Information Education Communication) and include health aspects such as cancer, women and child health, communicable diseases, HIV, adoption of children and many more. In controversial areas such as legislation and policies too, expert opinions are expressed through advertising—thus help maintaining freedom of expression to preserve ecology, heritage etc.

(xxiii) Advertising helps combat harmful propaganda

There are occasions when unfounded rumours affect organisations or misconceptions are aired by the ignorant or by vested interests. In such instances, corrective measures are taken and advertising too is used.

(xxiv) Advertising helps meet costs of most mass media

Without advertising revenue, the cost of an average newspaper would be several times the price we all pay. Media make available advertising space to advertisers in a cost effective manner and the revenue earned is used to subsidise the cost of media. This is to the benefit of the public too.

Through these and many other ways advertising is an integral part of our lives today and in a free economy, it will play its role even better.

Summary

Advertising has a key role to play in a free economy. Among other benefits, it provides choices to a consumer. Advertising benefits the advertiser, consumer and to an extent the society also. Most of the news and entertainment is supported by advertising economy of scale in production.

Globalisation of businesses are made easier through effective use of advertising. Advertising, as we discussed in this chapter has become an integral part of our lives.

Keywords

- Merchandise
- Cost-result ratio
- Customer-friendly offers
- Price competition
- Marginal territories
- Infringement
- Misconceptions
- Mass-production
- Clearing-house
- Discerning consumers
- Price wars
- Capital value
- Combat
- Generic products
- Obsolescence
- Destructive
- Smokes out
- Infringers
- Unfounded rumours

Discussion Question

1. Advertising results in increased cost of the product to the consumer. Will you agree with this? Justify your comment.

7

Role of Advertising Agency

7

The Advertiser and the Role of Advertising Agency

Advertising is a People Business

Advertising is aimed at people. Advertising is created by people. Advertising is paid for by people. How do we classify different people in advertising? What are their roles?

(i) The Customer

The customer is the person with the money to spend on products. Or it could be an organisation that requires capital equipment/raw material. Both the individual and the organisation alike are the customers.

Customers are of different types. One who is already a user, the second who is likely to buy and therefore a prospect and the third, who is unlikely to buy and is not a prospect.

Capital equipment, in the final analysis, depends on the masses. A freight ship, for example, may take raw materials, which are used by the importer for making goods. It is people who benefit any which way and directly or indirectly, customer means people.

(ii) The Advertiser

In today's equal opportunity environment, the advertiser is the person who promotes his product/service/idea to the customers. This person may be an individual who does all tasks from manufacturing to selling to advertising by himself, or it may be an organisation—a proprietary concern, a partnership, a private company, a limited company, a non-profit organisation and so on.

The advertiser for consumer goods used to say, "Advertising is aimed at your wife and she is no moron." Today it has to be amended to say, "Advertising is aimed at you and you are no fool." Even without testing this out, the aim is to make you open your wallet and spend money on the goods you need. Today, both the advertiser and the customer realise that through advertising happens value exchange.

Size and character of the organisation apart, the responsibility for directing the marketing communications would be that of one designated person. This person would have the qualifications and experience required for the job. As the organisation grows and becomes bigger, this person would have a designation, which would vary according to the organisation's culture. He could be just an Advertising Executive or Director of Advertising, or VP Marketing Communications, or this function could be the responsibility of the Marketing Head or Brand Head.

His function start with the variable P (Promotion) in Marketing. At the time a new product is considered or annual or semi-annual, long-term, short-term, test marketing etc., plans are undertaken, he gets involved in the overall planning and specifically takes over the functions of promotion. Naturally, he concerns himself with details—statistics, records, analysis, competitive information, data on markets, demographics, geographics, psychographics etc., of people, changes in taxation/legal areas that may have an impact and so on. He should have thorough knowledge of the target audience and the markets.

His is a management function with expertise in judging tailor-made creative and communication areas.

One of his functions is Return on Investment, or ROI as we call it. This is particularly essential in a highly competitive market where cost of advertising is escalating all the time. This escalation remains competitive (at per thousand audience as a measurable yardstick) but with media's audience increasing, so does the per unit rate of advertising. He has to get the very best value for the advertising money his organisation spends.

This person would work in tandem with related departments within the organisation, with the appointed advertising consultants and others. He should be able to "brief" the advertising agency and other creative people. The back-up needs of the company's sales force, the distribution chain etc., are to be taken care by him. He should also be able to impart training in marketing communication to others.

He should be a good planner and broadly, his job would include:

- Detailed and well planned budgets—for each product, for the year ahead, for advertising and sales promotion, as also for training etc.
- Supervising the work of the advertising agency and other experts.
- Liaison within his organisation.
- Decide on the marketing communications mix, media usage, schedules etc.
- Ensuring implementation of the programme as planned and at the same time be aware of sudden unforeseen changes that may warrant changes in strategy or even in the total planning.
- Undertake market research, tours to get feedback and to update his own knowledge, observe changes, competition etc., and also how the field force uses the support material given.
- Administer all his responsibilities, check and pass bills, ensure payments on time, prepare reports for the management on the impact of marketing communications for each aspect/product/market.
- In tandem with the sales people, monitor effect on targets and if achievement is below or above target, reasons why.
- Help in brand names, packaging etc.
- Communicate with everyone concerned so that maximum advantage is taken of the support given directly and indirectly to achieve targets.
- If a member of the industry associations, take active part.

This person would have adequate support staff and equipment such as computers, communication aids etc., and also a good database that would include the latest census, data on media, markets etc.

Like designation, there is no typical organisation structure for the Marketing Communications Department.

However, the following is illustrative and would give an idea of a structure (Fig. 7.1).

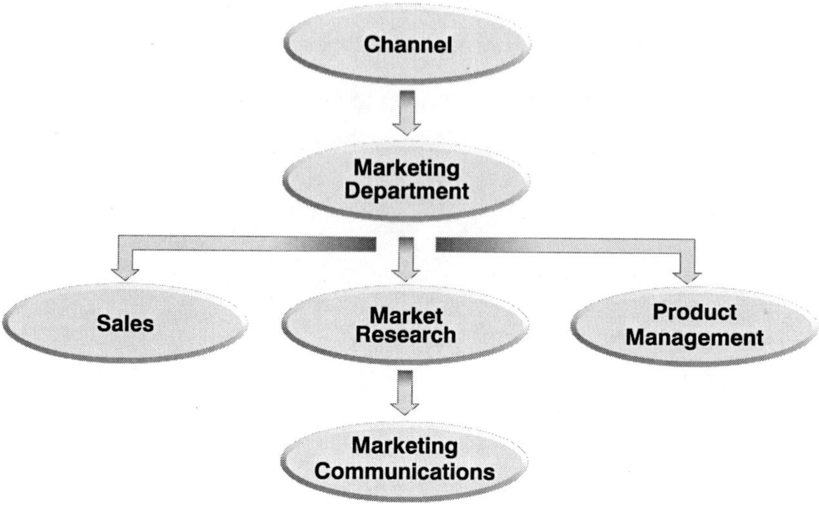

Fig. 7.1: Organisation structure for Marketing Communications Department

(iii) The Advertising Agency

The term "agency" has come into usage because, originally, the services were provided by an agent who would sell advertising space in newspapers, for a commission. Then the agent helped in writing the text for the advertisements and thus began the creative service. Thereafter, he had to engage artists to illustrate (photography had not arrived yet) and thus entered the first artists in advertising. With progress, the modern advertising agency is staffed and equipped to meet contemporary requirements.

What started as a one-man 'agent' role has blossomed into a specialised organisation, offering total services to clients. Advertising agencies (or consultants as they are better known) are run as business houses, some internationally, some nationally and some locally. The ownership could be held by a team of experts, a public limited company, or in some cases by advertisers (called house agencies), but they do work for other non-competing clientele too.

*(See the Appendices for some of the top agencies of India)

Agencies are chosen and 'appointed' by an advertiser and since there is a lot of confidentiality, the agencies are not expected to handle competitive business without the clearance of the principal. Talking of principal, the relationship between the advertiser and the agency is between two principals. (The agency does advertising on behalf of its client as a Principal with the Media which is also a Principal and in so doing, it is expected to pay the media on time irrespective of whether it gets paid by its client.)

Whether the advertiser goes directly to the media or uses the agency, the cost is the same. However, the agency is allowed a commission by the media. This is historical. In 1893, the American Newspapers Association resolved to allow 15% commission to advertising agents for services they rendered and not to allow any discount to the advertisers. This practice has been adopted by country after country and thus the agency gets a fixed income (commission) of 15% out of which it has to administer itself and also be liable for the media. In India, the Indian Newspaper Society "accredits" agencies and other media too recognise them and accord accreditation. Credit periods etc., are normally allowed only to the fully accredited agencies. If one were to study the economics of a good advertising agency, the gross it makes would be in the range of 1–1.5% the reason being its assets are the 'brains' it employs.

It is here that one should raise the question: How is it that some advertising works while it does not in many cases? Most marketing personnel (or entrepreneurs) think they know better than the seasoned professional with a track record. They also take the view that the agency should work for less than its fixed 15% commission. We have good products and also bad products. Similarly, we have good agencies and not so good ones. When principles need compromised, good ones opt out and the not so good ones cater to the whims and fancies of the client with the result the advertising created by them do not click. (There may be some lucky instances where it does though!) The better organisations believe that, just as their bottom line should show better profits, so should the agency that professionally contributes to that success. They respect the bottom line of the agency. Or, alternatively, they negotiate a "fee" for agency services, which may be even more than 15%.

It will also be interesting to see what happens to the 15% earned by the agency. It is the only income for the agency and since "brains" are employed, people are the agency's investment and asset. Agencies can be categorised as large, medium and small.

A study reveals this is what happens to every 15 rupees an agency earns:

	Manpower	Other expenses	Profit before tax
Large Agencies	11.50	2.81	0.69
Medium	10.50	2.73	1.77
Small	8.00	5.50	1.50

The profit before tax respectively for large, medium and small agencies would be 4.60%, 11.8% and 10% while the risk factor every agency faces is 25 times what they earn as gross in the case of large agencies and approximately 10 times in the case of medium and small agencies.

What is Agency's Function?

The first step is to get appointed for which the agency makes its profile known to the prospective client. After appointment, the agency has discussions with the client's management staff and others. This could be termed "briefing meetings" by the client and "contact meetings" by the agency. The agency records the discussions and forwards copies to the Principal.

Thereafter, the agency makes further studies on its own. It may interview customers, shopkeepers, opinion leaders etc.

The agency's functions could be summarised as:

- Ability to understand the advertiser's marketing plans and marketing problems.
- Ability to analyse and interpret these problems for the creative minds and media experts.
- Ability to evaluate and judge the creative ideas and to present these to the advertiser.
- Ability to prepare the ideal media strategy and plans.
- Ability to create ideas/advertising campaigns for the different media with the central idea as basic theme.
- Ability to produce reproduction material to suit each media.
- Ability to offer allied services such as help in positioning, advertising pre-and post-testing, packaging, public relations, and more.

The good agencies have structured themselves to meet the needs of diverse clientele and following table illustrates this:

CEO Business Development		
Creative Team	Operations Team	Support & Allied Services
Studio, Copy, Audio Visual etc.	Client Servicing/ Media (Planning) Media (Implementation)	Admin/HR Market Research
Production	Special Services: media buying, rural publicity etc. Branches	Accounts

There are core teams of experts within the agency (called the Plans Board) which discuss, analyse fine tune every little bit the agency does in terms of creatives, strategies and other services before presenting to the client.

(iv) Allied Services

Both the advertiser who may look after some aspects directly and the agency, which works on a client's behalf, require the services of specialists in diverse areas. Some of these are:

Printing	Various types of printing such as offset, screen, etc.
Outdoor	Signages, billboards, hoardings, banners, wall painting, neon, etc.
Vehicle Advertising	Buses, trains, etc.
Fabricators	Display items, models etc.
Market Research	Specialist organisations
Exhibitions	Specialists
Copy	Language/foreign languages copywriters
Typesetters	For language copy too
Models	For use in advertisements
Packaging	Experts in packaging
Photography	Industrial, fashion and so on
Audio Visuals	Film, audio visuals using tape, slides etc.,
Recording	for radio jingles etc.
Mailing	Direct mail services
Demos	House to house, in-shop demonstrations

Contd...

Rural market	Publicity vans, etc.
Window displays	Display specialists
Other media	Folk media specialists
Information	On competitors, syndicated researched ones etc.
e-marketing	Specialists
Telemarketing	Specialists
Direct marketing	Over TV etc.
Sponsorship	Sports, television serials and more.
Events	Event management groups

And many more such services including legal advisors, etc.

Summary

Advertising agency forms an important link between the advertiser and the media. The role of agency is to effectively communicate advertiser's messages to consumers through creative executions and use of cost effective channels for communication.

Advertising agency provides a spectrum of services to the advertiser. This allows the advertiser to focus on the core areas of marketing including product development, distribution management, customer service etc.

Advertising agency traditionally has been compensated with a commission of 15% on all media space/time. However, this is fast changing. Present trend is to link agency compensation with performance.

Keywords

- People business
- Escalation
- Accredited agencies
- Hoardings
- Radio jingles
- Event management
- Advertiser
- Tandem
- Briefing meetings
- Banners
- Publicity vans
- Billboards
- Return on investment
- Agency
- Contact meetings
- Wall painting
- Syndicated research
- Shop demonstrations

Discussion Questions

1. How should an advertiser select and evaluate performance of an advertising agency?
2. 'Commission method of compensating an agency is obsolete.' Discuss.

8

Advertising Planning

8

Advertising Planning

Advertising Uses Psychology

The most important people in marketing communications are consumers/prospects. Hence we should know all about the consumer and in particular psychological factors that would make him buy and use our product or services.

The Mind

What is mind? Where is the mind located? When people say they have a mind of their own, what does it mean? The exact location of the mind is a mystery but it is clearly associated with the brain and we know the exact location of the brain.

The brain is not an instrument of logic. As Albert Szent-Gyorgi has pointed out, "The human brain is not an organ of thinking but an organ of survival, like claws and fangs. It is made in such a way as to make us accept as truth that which is only to our advantage."You will notice that what we see or hear or smell are stored in different parts of the brain. We can recall what we read or hear word by word but cannot fully describe pictures or colours etc.

Advertising is Based on Psychology

Advertising, like Dale Carnegie's book, influences people and wins friends. Advertising aims at getting the brains of the audience to accept as truth the claims made and buy the product/idea/service. The successful adman will need the same qualities as a successful psychotherapist. Both need to be:

(i) Intelligent
(ii) Imaginative
(iii) Sensitive
(iv) Likeable
(v) Respected
(vi) Self-controlled
(vii) Flexible
(viii) Energetic

Both the adman and the psychotherapist aim at:

(i) Insight
(ii) Adoption to change
(iii) Attitude change
(iv) Behaviour change
(v) Relationship building

Both the adman and the psychotherapist are grossly different from the other professionals.

Since this is a people business, it should always be remembered that ALL PEOPLE DO NOT THINK ALIKE. The Indian professionals should understand that the discipline of Marketing and Marketing communications were developed in the West and brought into India by MNCs. Most of our efforts are in English (translated to other languages thereafter) and we assume all people, irrespective of their linguistic group, age etc., think alike. This is not so. There are innumerable cases where a name, a symbol etc., have been identified differently. (A radio was named Baron but in Tamil, the script is common for both B and P. Thus, in the transliteration, this became Paren (as in parent) and meaning grandson.

At this point, let us also realise that most of us can recall three things very fast and sometimes fourth one too. To illustrate, we say A B C, One Two Three, **Satyam Sivam Sundaram,** Land Sea Sky, **Tat tvam asi, Brahma Vishnu Siva,** etc., and in some cases ABCD—**Matha Pitha Guru Deivam** and so on.

Fig. 8.1: Creativity in advertising

Let us now look at how the mind, an associate of the brain, functions. It enables us to:

TO	THINK	FEEL	ACT

The mind is always in a state of flux. The mind is in a ceaseless, ever-changing parade of activity. This parade comprises sensations, perceptions, concepts, memories, judgment, thoughts, feelings, desires and so on. It is the mind that makes us conscious of all that happens around us and thus the mind is purposeful. It bestows on us the power to act, to exchange ideas, to create ideas, to formulate strength of character. Even the idle mind—a devil's workshop—is active but in a destructive way.

Modern psychology has postulated the existence of two kinds of mind:

(i) The Conscious Mind
(ii) The Unconscious Mind

There is a theory that there is a subconscious mind too, which is an intermediate and closer to the conscious stage of mind.

At the conscious level, we are vividly aware of certain thoughts and objects and the conscious mind consists of two areas : (a) The Focal and (b) The Marginal.

The focal idea is the very centre of consciousness, when our attention is most fully focused on the object/objects. The Marginal surrounds the focal field and contains elements of which we are only dimly aware. (like in a photograph, the object is in focus while the backdrop and props are not.)

The unconscious mind is the labyrinth of forgotten events and experiences. When we sleep, the mind does not and we do recall some of these. The subconscious mind is purely theoretical and given credence by psychoanalysts due to highly successful curative treatment in certain cases.

The Conscious and the Unconscious Mind Inter-play

Our conscious mind is constantly delving down into the unconscious, attempting to bring forgotten impressions into focus, recall memories and images into ever-new patterns of thoughts. Sometimes, several impressions, especially those gathered in early, formative years are pinned down in the depths of the unconscious. Though forgotten, these experiences remain clogged and block the free flow of mental process and adversely affect the self-expression and personality—and inversely, with efforts, help us overcome these blocks.

Mental Experience

What we experience through our minds consists of three distinct phases, which are:

(i) Conative (ii) Cognitive (iii) Affective

(i) Conative: It refers to the active, striving aspect of mental life and includes the process of doing things, that is, attention, impulsiveness, volition etc.

(ii) Cognitive: It refers to processes linked with knowing and thinking, and includes intellectual activities of the mind—memorising, creating, reasoning and the like.

(iii) Affective: It denotes the feeling qualities of the mind and include emotion, pleasure, pain and the like.

All three, however, interplay in the stream of our consciousness. For example, when we hear that a dear friend has received a special award (a) are delighted, which manifests affection **(Feel),** (b) the friend winning the award is an act of cognition **(Think)** and (c) we telephone or communicate to him in some way or the other our congratulations, which is an act of conation **(Act).**

Subjective Study of the Mind

Any intelligent person can study his own mind by introspection, which is also known as subjectivity. The person places himself as a third person and looks at himself as others would see him. The faculty of self-analysis is something to be developed through personal and sustained efforts.

Developing a subjective attitude will help a person engaged in marketing communications to look at his own work critically. For example, he likes an advertisement personally he would critically examine and question the headline, illustration, copy etc., as though he is a member of the audience. He would judge these asking, will the audience feel a desire for the advertised product/service? Is the advertisement persuasive enough? The quality of subjective judging is a must for a professional person. Most people take things for granted: for example, when the majority of the target audience possess black and white television, the professional, just because he is used to colour television, opts for something that may not be reproduced so well in black and white. A professional will always remember that advertising almost always touches the emotions of people and his own emotion has no place in judging what is right.

Objective Study of the Mind

This is based on objectives and relates to "other than the self", providing more definite results than the "introspective" subjective study. Objectivity falls into two divisions: One, the experience/knowledge gained by the past actions and second, experiments and other methods of observation used.

Mind and Body

The body movements and gestures are controlled by the mind. When one feels elated, one jumps with joy! Most of our emotions express themselves through physical behaviour. The mind and body are closely related and the saying "a healthy mind needs a healthy body" is true conversely too. The sensation, feel and how the mind works on our psyche are also to be observed.

Sensations

Sensations are simple, elementary processes of the mind. Of the many sensations including some in our nervous system or in the stomach etc., we readily think of five. These are:

• Eye	Visual
• Ear	Audible
• Nose	Olfactory
• Tongue	Gustatory
• Touch	Cutaneous

These five senses may also be classified under two headings: (i) Those concerned with our mental life, and (ii) Those concerned with our body activities.

In terms of recollection, sight and sound are more readily recalled than smell, taste and feeling of touch.

Wants

From the moment a child is born, there is want and these wants end only with death (even then, someone else has to spend for the funeral etc.) The modes of our experience are influenced by wants. This word, want, has tremendous import in marketing.

There are basic wants and there are psychological wants and some wants are acquired.

Psychologists have pointed out that there are some strong wants and that these are universal. All these however, are basic wants such as:

- Food
- Drink
- Security
- Shelter (freedom from fear)
- Companionship
- Welfare of loved ones
- Long, Healthy Life
- Superiority over others
- Social approval

These wants demand urgent satisfaction though the degree of urgency may vary from individual to individual. If we take food, the stone-age man had no option but to straightaway kill and devour his prey. We are civilised and have better options. However, even we would resort to theft if deprived of our normal civilised ways—this has been amply demonstrated in the 2005 hurricane disaster in Louisiana, America and the earthquakes in Jammu & Kashmir, India —because in both places relief was slow to reach.

There are acquired wants, also called secondary wants. In a civilised society, when we grow and mature, we become conscious of our position in the community and acquire aspects like taste, information, skill, leadership, style, efficiency, quality and so on. Secondary wants are not so quickly aroused as basic wants and as the nomenclature suggests, basic wants take precedence in our daily lives.

Drives

This can be illustrated with an example. A businessman was walking down a street at noon time. He had a very tiring morning and his mind was battling over a business problem. All of a sudden, he found himself entering a restaurant he rarely visited. He checked himself and realised it was lunch time, he was hungry and the smell of food wafting from this place drew him in. As he put it, "my nose knew better than my mind where I should go at that time." He was driven—psychologically—because he had to have food since a basic want, hunger, had set in and needed attention.

Drives need relief as quickly as is possible and scientifically, a drive is a condition of internal bodily tension that arises when an individual is deprived of something needed or wanted.

The point to remember is that drives motivate.

Motivation (Instincts)

A famous psychologist, McDougall, tells us that "Motivations are instincts which one sees in the physical and mental make-up of all humans and that every human being inherits psycho-physical tendencies from birth. That, with the growth of the human body, these tendencies become driving forces and determine the mode of behaviour and attitude to people and things in a society."

McDougall also defines instinct—"an inherited or innate psycho-physical disposition, which determines its possession, perceive and to pay attention to objects of a certain clear experience, an emotional excitement of a particular quality upon perceiving such an object and to act in regard to a particular manner—or at least experience an impulse to such action."

Under wants, we had listed eight basic ones. As against this list, McDougall outlines 14 instincts, which have accompanying emotions or instinctive activity. These are:

- Instinct for escape—from peril/danger/fear—real or imagined.
- Instinct for combat—associated with powerful emotion of anger.
- Instinct for appeal—when the instinct of combat fails and looks threatening the subject resorts to alternative means such as looking for support or rescue by the audience/friends/relatives/law etc. This also includes bluffs such as warning of consequences and the like.
- Instinct for repulsion—this is discernable when one is offended by an experience (say bad smell/taste) or thought. The emotion is one of disgust.
- Instinct for parenting—Love of children by parents is a tender emotion when man forgets all aggressive tendencies.
- Instinct for mating—This is basically sexual and according to Dr. Sigmund Freud, this instinct predominates all actions in life.
- Instinct for curiosity—This relates to the thirst for knowledge, for imagination and corresponding emotion is awe, wonder.
- Instinct for submission—This is negative self-feeling. Unavoidable in the presence of teachers, parents, great men and even the thought of God.
- Instinct for self-assertion—Showing off, smiling triumphantly etc. The emotion is positive and one of well-being.

- Instinct for gregariousness—Getting together with other people, friends, families including in parties, weddings and the like. A sense of belonging, friendship, cooperation etc., develops. The emotion of loneliness compels people to seek gregarious activities.
- Instinct for food—Feeling of hunger and urgent drive urges this instinct, often in the same day.
- Instinct to acquire—This started with hoarding food in the early days and today manifested in our shopping, savings, etc. A feeling of 'ownership' develops.
- Instinct to construct—This is an expression of creative work—doing something worthwhile, organising, building up, leadership etc.
- Instinct for laughter—An emotion of amusement and this leads to our search for entertainment/pleasure.

Motivation for Action Arises from Deep Urges and Emotion

Basic wants apart, human instincts are influenced by (a) the country and the race one belongs to and (b) experience-satisfaction and (c) the society we now live in. Some aspects are:

Habit

The kind of life we lead today has evolved over a period of time. Along with our progress from generation to generation, our survival still depends on our native instinct to act spontaneously to preserve our species in time of danger and uncertainty. Native instincts plus the activities we have learnt to acquire, together form the fundamental driving force or, what we can call, a "purpose."

The learnt activities form our habits. Some reactions such as emotion, joy, fear, sorrow etc., are not always passed on and, because of maturity levels, are controlled. By so doing, we acquire "conduct" through habits like behaviour in public and shape ourselves as part of a civilised society. Often times, this kind of restrained conduct can be highly frustrating too. A heavy smoker would certainly feel frustrated on a journey by plane or trains or even buses—because smoking is banned. He becomes uncomfortable, fidgety, edgy and his uneasiness can some times be visible.

Habits lie at the foundation of character and personality. Good habits develop strength of character and bad ones the opposite. Habits are inculcated from childhood and our way of speaking, eating, drinking, walking dressing, our manners—all are implanted in us during our formative years. It is said that an individual's basic habits are firmly rooted in his personality by the time he reaches the age of 22.

New Habits: When new habits are to be popularised, psychologists recognise repeated efforts as an essential factor. Many brands that are market leaders began as something new and the organisations behind this attached great importance to repeated efforts including marketing communications. They have been promoting consistently for decades. They have recognised that habit-forming advertising is a full-time, long-term continuous effort—and over time, a continuing permanent effort of the organisation. Not long ago, the custom in our country, when visitors arrived, was to offer a glass of water/some buttermilk etc. Today it is a branded soft drink because of the new habit-encouraging advertising as part of today's lifestyle.

The influence of habit and habit-encouragement is very strong. The advertiser recognises this factor and accordingly shapes his product/ message. Advertising encourages a social value of habits. Our own judgment of others is based on their good and indifferent or bad traits. Habit has a key place in our social interactions/relationships especially in the work environment. It is a truism that those who are accustomed to do work that we call drudgery willingly carry on regardless of low remuneration, whilst those accustomed to more congenial forms of work tend to be different. Also, with promotions and upgrades, people do get to resent the conditions under which they had earlier worked.

Feelings/Emotions

How a person will feel depends on what he reads, sees, hears. Feelings are with each one of us at every moment of our waking life. These are either pleasurable or painful and one's state of feeling is mirrored in his expressions. By and large. a smiling countenance is likely to evoke a pleasant feeling(and response), which is why most magazines carry pictures of smiling, happy models/sports people etc., on the cover page.

Emotion is more specific even though it emanates from feelings. Normally, emotion is associated with some bodily 'movement' or activity, however slight or extensive.

Emotion is also associated with glandular and circulatory changes, which affect muscular activities. When in fear or anger, adrenal glands become more active, the liver rapidly releases stored sugar into the blood. Blood circulation is quickened. In civilised life, emotions are not always allowed free display and may often stop, may be with a clenched fist and the like.

Sentiment

The mental process, which systemises emotions, could be described as sentiment. This is manifest, for example, in the love/affection of one's own birthday/wedding anniversary etc., or the love for a pet animal or the sense of belonging to an organisation, an educational institution (school tie/alumni), a club and so on.

Emotion and sentiment do build character and the self-regarding sentiment is concerned with one's own personality. This is what makes one feel bad or good when he does something and is of great importance for the development of a controlled and balanced personality.

Pictures

A Chinese proverb succinctly describes a picture, 'A picture is worth a thousand words.' Pictures speak a universal language, are understood readily by people—even the illiterates—because pictures do not require special training to understand. They do have tremendous ability to express thoughts in the simplest form and get attention easily.

Repetition

We observed earlier—under New Habits—that repetition is important, especially when new habits are to be propagated. To get a brand name or an idea registered in the minds of people, it is important to study the 'memory' process of people. Such a study, social scientists tell us, would reveal to us conditions under which memory can be aided or under which it is handicapped.

People tend to forget and this is also a key reason why repetition is essential—they need to be constantly reminded until it becomes a habit.

Memory and Association

The principle of associating two words or ideas with one another is common in marketing communications. For example, one would recall Colgate that always carries the Brand name along with the product—as Colgate Toothpaste. It is the same with Close Up and other brands. Associating brand name with the product and repeatedly exposing this to the users is perhaps the best means of creating a vivid memory and guarding against forgetting.

Summary

Advertising is all about psychology. The mind is the focus for the communication strategist. Our mind consists of three distinct areas, which are: Cognitive, Affective and Conative.

Cognitive refers to process linked with knowing and thinking. Affective refers to emotions, preferences for a brand. Conative refers to the process of willingness to buy.

In communication we use five sensations: Eye-visual, Ear-Audible, Nose-Olfactory, Tongue-Gustatory, Touch-Cutanous. In terms of recollection sight and sound are more readily recalled than smell, taste and feeling of touch. It is for this reason that advertising uses more frequently sight and sound sensations.

Psychologists have identified some basic needs which are satisfied through products and services. Theory of learning helps us understand how individuals learn to use products, dispose them appropriately etc.

Keywords

- Conscious mind
- Unconscious mind
- Subconscious mind
- Motivation
- Instincts
- Sensations
- Wants
- Drives
- Emotion
- Habits
- Sentiments
- Cognitive component of mind
- Affective component of mind

Discussion Questions

1. Discuss the three areas of the mind which determine the ultimate behaviour of a consumer.
2. Discuss various instincts and their application in marketing.

9

Setting Objectives

9

Setting Objectives

In 1954, the late Peter Drucker presented Management by Objectives, or MBO as a concept. This highlighted the need for objectives to be arrived at in clear and measurable terms, preferably against some previously established standard.

The objectives need to be clear, concise and with a time frame for accomplishing.

MBO also involves participation both from bottom up and top down the line. Thus it ensures that the managed and the management both develop a commitment—based on clearly enunciated goals. Participation in developing the goals is a commitment by the participants and thus includes everyone—the junior, the manager, the top management. There are nine benefits derived by applying MBO:

(i) Concrete objectives can direct PERFORMANCE.

(ii) Concrete objectives can reduce UNCERTAINTY.

(iii) Concrete objectives can serve as an INSTRUMENT OF COMMUNICATION.

(iv) MBO can point out where greater coordination between managers is needed. As an example, one marketing unit may have to cut down its request for budget money in order that another unit can have a little more money.

(v) MBO can change the role of a superior from being a judge evaluating subordinates, to a role of facilitator, counsellor and encourager.

(vi) MBO can provide subordinates with the latitude and freedom to make decisions without always checking first with superiors for approval.

(vii) MBO can lead to improved planning—because, the manager knows what his subjects are as well as the expectations of his superiors.

(viii) MBO can produce a shift from control over people to control over operations. Managers are therefore judged on how well they manage and coordinate operations.

(ix) MBO can generate more immediate response to deviations from standards. The manager, without compromising quality, knows the objectives and priorities.

Setting Objectives for Marketing Communications

The most demanding exercise is the situation analysis, which forms the basis for everything else that needs to be done in developing marketing communications. This is all the more important since such communications mean expenditure. Such expenditure could be converted into investment for achieving goals or in simpler language, obtain Return On Investment.

In a MBO situation, the top management is concerned with long-term objectives while the brand management level is concerned with day-to-day operations with the other levels in between forming a chain. The relative importance should be obvious—and is shown in the following lines:

- Top management sets organisation's objectives and gives directions down the line.
- There are, by implication, contracts for performance and such contracts are within the set objectives (these are not written down but implied contracts).
- There is an in–built evaluation process of performance at every stage.
- Evaluation serves as input for the next set of objectives.
- Better accountability is established.

Setting marketing communications objectives therefore is a sound way of assessing the degree of success or otherwise. In any event, setting objectives narrows down the strategies that follow the situation analysis, especially in the areas of message, media, promotions and, more importantly, in eliminating poor strategy options that may have no chance of allowing the organisation to meet its objectives.

Objectives, as we observed earlier, help set directions. Without objectives and directions, the situation could well be what Alice and the Cheshire Cat (C.Cat) faced:

Alice: "Will you please tell me, please, which way I ought to go from here?"

C.Cat: "That depends a good deal on where you want to go."

Alice: "I don't much care where...."

C cat: "Then it does not matter which way you go."

Alice: "So long as I get somewhere."

C Cat: "Oh! You're sure to do that if you only walk long enough."

Starting on Setting Marketing Communications Objectives

What does marketing communications (Advertising and Sales Promotion) mean? How does one define this? Colley, the author of Defining Advertising Goals for Measured Advertising Results—DAGMAR for short—has defined Marketing Communications as:

"A specific communication TASK
to be accomplished among a defined AUDIENCE
to a given DEGREE
in a period of TIME."

In this definition, there are four components, namely

(i) Task
(ii) Audience
(iii) Degree (of change)
(iv) Time (time frame)

We shall now look at these components:

(i) Task

The marketing communications expert employed by the organisation (or whoever is in charge of this department and this could be the Marketing Chief himself or a brand executive) needs to set the task for marketing communications. What precisely would be this task? Such a task could obviously be within the hierarchy effects of communications such as creating awareness, knowledge, preference, trial purchase and repeat purchases.

If we take awareness, what would be the objective? Would the percentage of awareness aimed among the target audience be 100% or would it be less or 80% or 60%? This needs to be spelt out.

Similarly, what would be percentages for knowledge, preference and so on?

What should be the task in terms of purchases by prospects? In the case of trial purchase, to what extent can marketing communications aim at closing an instant sale?

Would the marketing communications function perform the complete selling function too? Could it sell to the already pre-disposed prospect? Could it announce a compelling special rationale? Or would it merely remind people to buy?

Would the communication be restricted to special occasions/season e.g., Diwali or Christmas or New Year? How would it stimulate impulse sales?

Would it be a near-term effort—create brand image/favourable emotional disposition/implant information/attitude regarding superiority?

What would be its role? To combat competition or to overcome competitive claims? Or to correct false impressions, misinformation and so on?

There could be a combination of tasks too such as liquidating current model/fashion and introducing new ones or some other combinations.

What would be the long-term tasks?

The professional needs to zero in on the right question as applicable to the situation, product life cycle, competition, changes in taste and many more questions that are revealed through the situation analysis.

(ii) Audience

The marketing of goods or services or ideas is primarily and ultimately to the specific audience. The more precisely one knows who comprises the audience, the easier it becomes to set objectives. Such audience could be a family, housewives, the young at heart, the elderly, festive shoppers, health oriented people, investors, etc.

Defining audience is so important that it is part of situation analysis. The segmentation/clear description of the audience or audiences by priority must be clearly stated. The audience need to be unambiguously defined on the basis of usage and thereafter on the basis of enduring demographics (sex, age group, occupation, income etc.) geographics (place of living or if travelling, specific places), followed by psychographic (lifestyle) traits.

(iii) Degree of Change

What is the degree of change one targets? This should be spelt out in terms of : User segment, Share of the market, Attitude to the product, Attitude to competition, Buying habits, etc.

This input impacts the advertising budget as also the character of the marketing communications.

(iv) Time Frame

Neither the tide nor the competition will wait and it is of paramount importance to pin point the time elements proposed in all the aspects of communications. At what point of time would goals be met?

Before the advent of marketing discipline in the 1960s, time frames for new products extended to even five years for a market share. Among some product lines such as cough mixture, there is no defined market leader at any time—because of seasonality perhaps, every season, this field witnesses marketing communications different from the regular advertising.

The time frame for a new product today can also be divided and stated task-wise, as in the following example:

(a) 95% awareness within the first three months among the target audience.

(b) 85% interest, predisposition to the brand in the same period.

(c) 75% trial purchase within the next three months.

(d) 85% (of the 75% in number 3 above) repeat purchase within the next two months. (Or, increase the target audience from 75% to 85%).

After the introductory stage of three months, the communication mix could change to include sales promotion in order to accelerate trial and thereafter repeat purchase or after achieving 75% trial purchase without incentives, the task could be to raise the numbers to 85% through sales promotion.

Marketing Communications vs Marketing Objectives

In most situations, it is difficult to distinguish between marketing goals and marketing communication objectives. The most popular and prevalent method is stating the marketing objective alone—such as 35% of the market share in the first twelve months and this objective is also set as the communications objective.

In practice, the achievement of goals would be the sum total of several factors and inputs: price, product, performance, distribution, branding etc., while marketing communications needs to motivate customers by first creating awareness, then desire and lead to trial and repeat purchases. Marketing communications, apart from imparting these, can also influence buyer's behaviour. In the long run, marketing communications will succeed if all the other elements are in place. These are the reasons why the situation analysis dwells on marketing and corporate objectives per se.

Schools of Thought

In this context, there are two schools of thought, called, for convenience, the Sales School and the Communication Effect School on what marketing communications should do.

The Sales School feels that the only meaningful goal must be that marketing communications ought to directly influence sales.

The Communication Effect School, on the other hand, states that the consumer must move through the hierarchy of effects towards purchase and therefore marketing communications ought to work in combination with other variables in the marketing mix in order to achieve sales.

If we want to evaluate the two claims, we will need to look at the question of measurement of tasks. It is easy to measure sales rather than degree of awareness, interest, disposition, preference, trial etc. With research techniques improving all the time, good marketing organisations undertake continuous research on all aspects of marketing including the effectiveness of marketing communications.

Because of this methodology in working, better organisations ensure that people at all levels have a clear idea of what they are aiming at. The people in the team therefore process and deal with the appropriate issues.

Setting clear objectives also helps the "creators" of communications (who normally work within narrow parameters, their views restricted to their own fields) to get involved and work to a given statement of objectives. The media strategists and planners too get benefited.

Working with clear objectives thus helps in avoiding wastage of efforts, to focus on right ideas instead of bright ideas. Right solutions evolve instead of bright ones.

Setting objectives is not only for marketing communications. This exercise needs to be done for all aspects of the marketing mix, in clear terms. This will give correct directions to achieving targeted results.

Summary

Success of any communication programme to a large extent will depend on clearly defined objectives. Late Peter Drucker presented Management By Objectives or MBO as a concept. This concept is as relevant in advertising as in any other field of business management.

Prof Colley the author of Defining Advertising Goal for measuring Advertising results—DAGMAR for short—has defined marketing communications as "a specific Communication task to be accomplished among a defined a udiences to a given degree in a period of time."

There are two schools of thought on marketing communication objectives: the Sales School and the Communication Effect School.

The Sales School approaches objectives in communication to impact changes in sales—market share, volume etc.

The Communication Effect School on the other hand states that the job of communication is to take the the prospects through the hierarchy of effects before achieving the sales.

Keywords

- MBO
- DAGMAR
- The Sales School
- The Communication Effect School

Discussion Question

1. Discuss DAGMAR approach to managing communication objectives.

10

Positioning: Creative Planning

10

Positioning: Creative Planning

Advertising Campaigns

In advertising campaign is a series of advertisement messages that share a single idea and theme which make up an integrated marketing communication (IMC). Advertising campaigns appear in different media across a specific time frame. Various types of media can be used in these campaigns such as radio, TV and Internet.

Radio and TV advertising campaigns use methods including but not limited to electronic billboards, commercial announcements, personal endorsements, promotions, blurbs and plugs. Radio and TV Advertising Campaigns can also utilize Direct Response Advertising, Viral Marketing and Remnant Advertising, as well as include newer technology such as Satellite advertising.

Much like Satellite radio, Internet advertising campaigns can be viewed as a more recent development based on the advancements of technology and the growing availability of Internet throughout the world. Methods used in Internet advertising include but are not limited to search engines, banners, blurbs, video clips, interactive games and emails. Campaigns can also utilise Direct Response Internet Advertising, Viral Advertising, and Remnant Internet Advertising.

Marketing departments and advertising agencies might utilise one or any number of different media types as well as advertising methods. Others will focus on one form of medium and/or specialise in one or two particular methods of advertising.

The critical part of making an advertising campaign is determining a campaign theme, as it sets the tone for the individual advertisements and other forms of marketing communications that will be used. The campaign theme is the central message that will be communicated in the promotional activities. The campaign themes are usually developed with the intention of being used for a substantial period but many of them are short lived due to factors such as being ineffective or market conditions and/or competition in the marketplace and marketing mix.

Advertising campaign is an attempt to reach a particular target market by designing a series of advertisements and placing them in various advertising media. In other words, advertising campaign is series of advertisement messages that share a single idea and theme which make up an integrated marketing communication (IMC). Advertising campaigns appear in different media across a specific time frame.

Elements of a Successful Advertising Campaign

A successful marketing campaign needs certain elements to be successful. The following information will help you to develop a successful marketing campaign.*

(i) Establish a feeling of urgency for the buyer

Basically tell your customers, "You need to sign up today because it will make you reach your goals." Don't tell your customer the offer will still be as good tomorrow; they must buy today! Urgency! Study how successful ads make the customer act now.

(ii) Show a list of benefits

There must be a list of benefits to make customers sign up. Will you be smarter using your services? Will he get more visitors? Will your server be better than the competitions hardware? Will your business help to make the site more successful? Or make him richer, or healthier, or faster? Focus on the client, not the advertiser. Most benefits need to be skillfully integrated into the ad. It is a waste of time and money in an ad or on your website if you do not work in benefits and present them properly.

(iii) Call to action

Tell them what they must do to get it. Do not assume that your prospects and customers will figure out how to get what you are offering. They will not do your work for you. So, go ahead and tell them what to do. If they have to call you to get it, then tell them to

*See appendix for top 100 advertising campaigns

call (to call you now!). If they have to write or drop a postcard in the mail, or fax something to you, then tell them clearly and in words easy to understand. The point is to make it as easy as possible for your target customer to do what you want them to do. People do not like to do anything that is going to take work on their part. Make it as easy for them to respond as possible, or they will not = no good results for you.

(iv) Do it again

You have to (must) tell customer what to do (to sign up with you). Tell your customer to order now (this moment). So many ads assume that the customer will guess to fill out the contact us form, e-mail you, or telephone for the information, or product. Tell the customer what to do. Provide the customer on how to respond today in several ways. As more options you can offer, the better will be the results.

(v) Plan your advertising calendar and campaign several months in advance

Failure to plan advertising in advance will waste a lot of your money. Rush charges, poor design, rate increases, poor creative and poor copy are common results of failing to plan in advance. "I didn't have enough time", "I was under the gun to get this placed", are common phrases heard under rushed circumstances. Take a blank calendar and fill in the days, months, or quarters to advertise to your target markets. Figure out the number of ad insertions that will make sense and negotiate a contract with the various media suppliers (e.g., local newspapers). Book banner web space on the important website early in advance. Prepare your website with a special landing page for the expected visitors.

(vi) Test your banners and your ads

Only by trial and error will you be able to set a baseline as to the best response rates for your ads and banners. It is very important to maximise response for the amount of dollars spent. Sometimes re-phrasing text or adjusting the ad layout can make the difference between a low or just average response and a great success and high ROI (Return on Investment). You will need to find out what works best for your business. After you find this out, you will want to stay on course and base future advertising campaigns on the success of the old one.

(vii) **Avoid misleading or dishonest advertising**

Avoid misleading or dishonest advertising in hopes of converting duped readers/website visitors into using your products or services. Honesty and integrity are the primary key to repeat sales and repeat business. If you have to trick your audience to get their attention, you will have a very hard time keeping their attention and their business if they sign up at all.

(viii) **Running on (web)site events**

Running events on your website is an excellent way to encourage repeat traffic and repeat visitors. You will want to begin running events once traffic from your site launch begins to fade. Examples include contests, games, on-line interviews, chat sessions and maybe even audio broadcasts. Do the things your competitors do not do.

Creative Strategies in Advertising

In **advertising,** different **creative strategies** are used in order to obtain consumer attention and provoke shoppers to purchase or use a specific brand . Advertisers use different ways of thinking to create catchy slogans that capture consumer attention. Creative strategies promote publicity, public relations, personal selling and sales promotion.

These ways of thinking are divided into three basic descriptions: Weak strategies, mid-strength strategies and strong strategies. The strategies labeled "strong, mid-strength, and weak are generic phrases used in the textbooks referenced below to help students understand the intensity of each different type of advertising strategy. Advertisements, weak, mid-strength, and strong can be found in television, radio, and magazines/print."

Since the beginning of advertising, strategies have been created, starting with the simplest (weak) strategies in the 1940s.

Weak Strategies

Generic and pre-emptive strategies describe the two weakest forms of advertising that were most popular through the 1940s.

- A generic strategy gives a product attribution. An example of this would be how the beef industry chose to advertise their product. With their slogan, "Beef, it's what's for dinner," consumers are not learning anything new about the product.

- The Beef slogan simply states beef as a dinner item. It enhances the product in no other way.

A pre-emptive strategy is a form of advertising that makes a generic claim stronger. An example of a pre-emptive strategy can be found in Folgers Coffee. As many of us know, most coffee is grown in the mountains. Folgers took that fact and claimed it as their own with their slogan, "Folgers: Mountain Grown Coffee."

Middle-strength Strategies

The mid-strength strategies have unique positioning strategy, brand image and positioning.

"Previously called USP or Unique Selling Proposition" and a continue unique positioning strategy is proving that something about your product is truly unique. This is commonly found when producers take an average product and add a new, unique element to it. An example of Unique Positioning Strategy would be in Crest toothpaste. Crest added the unique feature of Scope in their product to differentiate it from other brands of toothpaste.

- A downfall in Unique positioning strategy advertising is that if a unique feature increases sales on one product, many other brands are likely to adopt the "unique" feature, making the end product not so unique.

Positioning is one of the most important excersises in creating advertising. It was developed in the 1970s and is still widely used today. In positioning one brand will take its product and "position" it against a competing product.

- An example of positioning can be found in the rental car company Avis slogan. With The Hertz car company being the leader in rental car services, Avis took their number two position and used it to their advantage by creating the slogan, "When you're number two, you try harder."

Brand Image is another very common way companies choose to advertise. In brand image, an advertiser is not trying to create rational thinking. This type of advertising strives to create emotion and give a brand a personality. A common way of doing this is by using a celebrity as a spokesperson.

- A great example of brand image is found in Proactive Acne Solutions. In each of their commercials they have celebrities sharing their Proactive experiences, giving the brand a face people want to be.

Strong strategies

The third and strongest form of creative strategy includes affective advertising and resonance advertising.

Making people feel really good about a product is called 'affective advertising'. This is difficult to do, but often humour and an honest character can make affective advertising possible.

- A great example of affective advertising is found in the "Geico" commercials. By creating a friendly, honest, funny gecko as a spokesperson, consumers tend to trust what the gecko is saying and find humour in his actions. This creates a good feeling about the actual service "Geico" offers.

Lastly, resonance advertising is a way of identifying with consumers. If an advertiser can create a campaign that certain target markets identify with, then resonance advertising has been achieved.

- An example of resonance advertising is in "Tide" detergent ads. Many times mothers are busy doing laundry in between sports practices and driving their children around in mini vans. Their recognition with soccer moms makes "Tide" a favourite pick among women with children who are very involved in activities.

POSITIONING With these examples in developing marketing communications, sequentially, we now look at positioning. What is positioning? Ayer's Dictionary on advertising terms defines this thus:

"The art and science of fitting the product or service to one or more segments of the broad market in such a way as to set it meaningfully apart from competition".

The idea of positioning was pioneered and popularised by a team of two people, Ries and Trout. To them, Positioning refers to:

"The image in the minds of the consumer that is created by relating the firm's brand to one or more competitive brands."

In actual practice, to succeed at a position the brand must not just relate to competition or if it is a first of its kind, relate to earlier uses, but must do so with reference to a unique and meaningful benefit. A researcher, Knabler, presented four simple but important rules concerning perceptions in the market place as against a position that exploits consumer perceptions of a unique and meaningful benefit in the product class. The four rules postulated by Knabler are:

(i) If consumers are not users or potential users, they are of no concern to the firm. Position is related to the target market (alone) and therefore we should be concerned with actual users and their perceptions—what benefit they derive from the product and their views thereof. (If one were asked to name the best in cars, the name Rolls Royce would emerge, but how many people do really buy this brand or can afford to? Such a position is of no use amongst the not so rich.)

(ii) If a user does not believe that a product characteristic is indeed a benefit, to them it is not a benefit at all. Therefore the perceptions of the management are not relevant at the point of decision making by customers. (A lower middle class house builder may just not be interested in marble or Italian tiles for his flooring and these benefits mean nothing to him.)

Attributes vs Benefits

It should be remembered that the perception of the organisation (advertiser) is based on Attributes. The consumer, on the other hand, perceives on the basis of benefits. No consumer buys attributes. He buys only benefits. Therefore attributes must be transformed and translated into benefits in a meaningful manner. A simple example would be automobiles. All cars have wheels, suspensions, shock absorbers etc. These are 'attributes'. What the buyer of a car perceives is a 'Smooth ride'. The positioning here is based on smooth ride and the attributes are offered as reasons.

(iii) If the benefit itself is unimportant to the customer, it has no significance. Perceptions of the consumers are all encompassing. Therefore perceptions need to be culled out of multi-attributes models.

As an example, (fictitious example) let us look at attributes of a small car and let us also assume there are five competing brands in the market. The importance scale of the attributes could be 0 to 10 with a minimum ranking by customers at say 6:

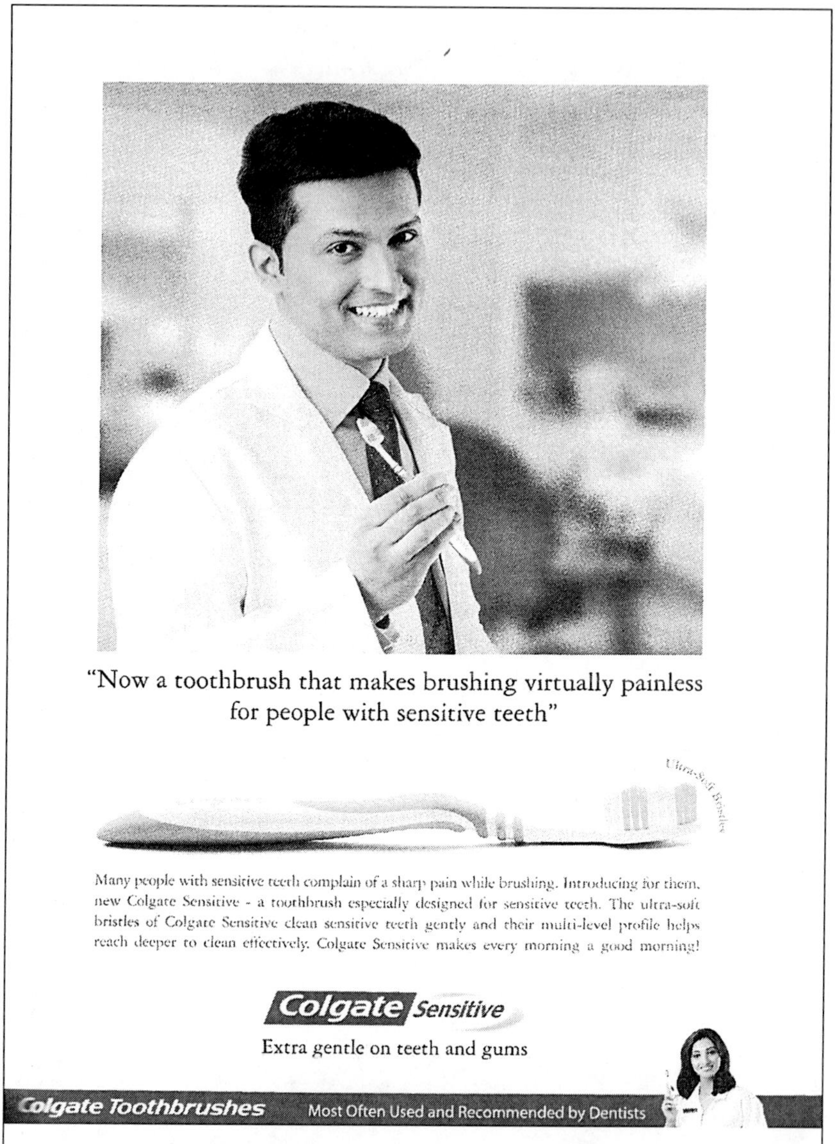

Fig. 10.1: Colgate uses Benefit Positioning

Brands are A, B, C, D and E

Attribute:	5	6	7	8	9	10
Mileage		C	DA		BE	
Price		D	E		A B C	
Performance		A D E		C	D	
Style		ED	A	B	C	
Comfort		A	ED		C	B
Others*						

(others:*example Installment Sale, Insurance etc., all are the same.)

An analysis would reveal that Brand B scores overall and also on specific issues. Even then a claim that "ours is a car that has won the Indian Desert Rally or the Most Spiffy designed car" would not have the same perception as performance, style, mileage etc., with the consumer.

(iv) **Positioning** is based on difference as perceived and should also take into reckoning the far too many competing advertisements vying for attention and for the same expenditure from the customer, the clutter, the clashing claims, the multiplicity of brands. Therefore, the message must ideally be associated with something to which customers can relate. New messages tend to be rejected if they differ from perceptions that exist. Therefore POSITIONING is built on WHAT EXISTS IN CONSUMERS' PERCEPTIONS.

Positioning: Building Brand Asset

Positioning, in simple terms, is an exercise to capture the top slot in the mind's of the target audience. In our daily lives, if one is asked to name the world's highest peak, the name of Everest is the spontaneous answer. To name the fourth or fifth highest is not at all easy.

- Some positioning examples:
- Every one has a reason to pray: Cycle Pure Agarbati
- It's God's own country: Kerala

- Utterly Butterly AMUL (developed for Amul Butter, it is difficult to offer the same line for Amul Cheese or Chocolate and other Amul products)
- Dhoodh se safedhi (whiter than milk) : Nirma
- Where there is Lifebuoy there's health. Where there's health there's Lifebuoy: Lifebuoy

Over a period of time, the investment in building brands and a position for these brands in the "minds" of the customers pay dividends and once built, it is very difficult to dislodge them.

When all carbonated sodas are similar, it is positioning that makes people prefer a brand name, be it Coke, Pepsi, Limca, Thums Up etc., or if it is a health drink, people go for Complan, Horlics and Boost.

Over the years, brand names become very strong and powerful. Manufacturers of allied items (to which the original brand/the owner of the brand does not diversify), pay huge royalties for using that name. Cigarette lighters named after famous Cigarattes used to be common. Wristwatches too are named similarly.

What does a brand that does not enjoy the number one positioning slot in the minds of people do to get their attention and convert them to its consumers? Sometimes a perceived weakness can be turned into advantage. As said earlier Hertz Rent-a-car enjoys the number one position and Avis, the number two frankly admits this—"We are No.2 and therefore we try harder." Miller Light Beer acknowledges that other beers contain more calories. Volkswagon acknowledges that other cars are prettier, bigger.

All these brands (and there are many more) instead of attacking the leader, acknowledge the leader more or less on the lines of Anthony (in Julius Ceaser) exhorting all Romans,—"They' are all honorouble men."

Developing Positioning that Lead to Strategies

The positioning for any brand must necessarily be built upon facts gathered through the situation analysis. It is equally necessary to identify competition, not only in terms of overall strengths and weaknesses, but also how competition is perceived by the consumers as well as their positioning.

Analysing the data would lead to (a) finding a niche, (b) developing brand position. When Vicks was introduced, against the unassailable Amrutanjan as a pain balm, Vicks chose to promote itself as a cold rub. Nirma, though low priced, took the position of whiter than milk washes against Surf and Rin.

We also need to seek answers to questions such as :

"Can one category position the brand? The positioning for the brand seeks one role, where there is good potential. A good example would be Maggie noodles—as an instant snack food. Maggie is better recalled with "Just two minutes."

Can positioning be on a selling idea? This question is broken further as:

Product oriented: One attribute. Example: Complan as a complete planned food.

Consumer oriented: We have already cited Lifebuoy as an example. Wah Taj for Brooke Bond tea can be another.

All these positions are so well entrenched in the minds of people, both consumers and others, they are difficult to imitate (copy) or when someone tries to imitate, the consumer immediately recalls the original brand. In the 1950s, Dettol was promoted as "Kills invisible germs." When Savlon was launched by ICI, people who did not have the habit of using antiseptic, instead of trying Savlon, opted for Dettol—which later on became generic with antiseptics as such. Sales of Dettol increased!

There are other forms of positioning too.

Commercial Positioning: Here, the total effect of words, picture, product-brand, all convey a meaning. For example, Marlboro Cigarettes sold the "individuality" of Americans via illustrating wide open spaces, a horse and rider, with the cigarette pack at the centre. The total effect became the positioning, be it outdoor or print or cinema.

Positioning by Attribute: Burnol for burns, Anacin for pain relief and so on are examples of attribute-related positioning.

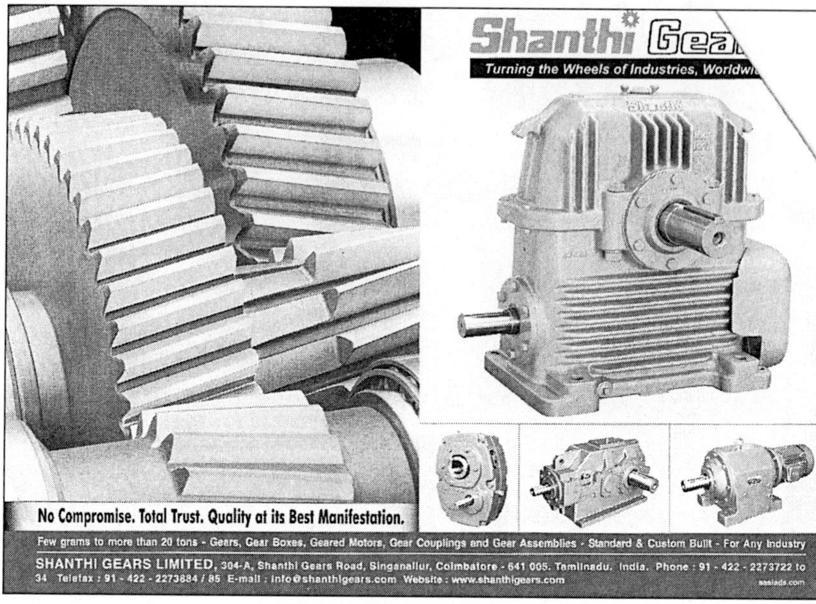

Fig. 10.2: Industries quality

Positioning by Application: M Seal, Fevicol etc., are excellent examples.

Positioning by Product User: The children used by Johnson & Johnson for their baby products/nappies for children and so on.

Positioning by Product Class: DHL Couriers, Lufthansa Airlines make good examples.

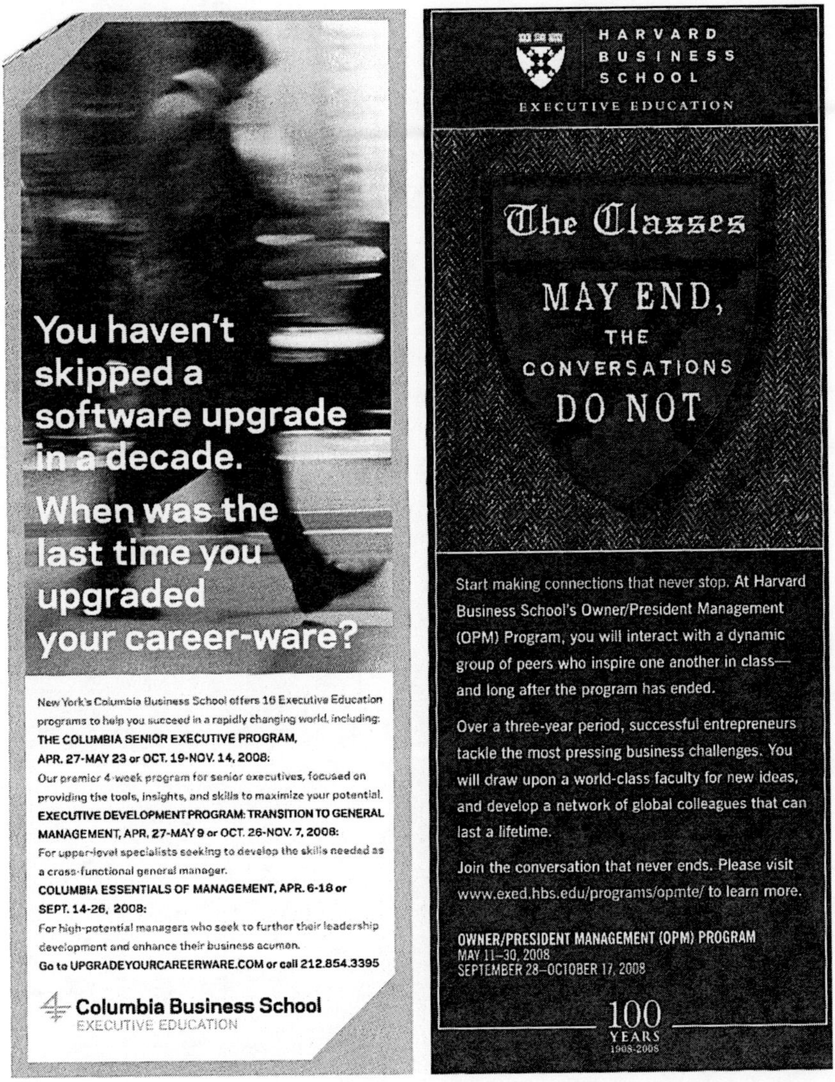

Fig. 10.3: Business and software career

Positioning in relation to Competition: Admitting one is not all that big as the leader but at the same time slighting the competition. A good example is Onida: "Owners Pride, Others envy"; Santro as the Zip Car and so on.

Fig. 10.4: Electronic Selling

Some products such as "M&M is a candy that melts in your mouth, not in your hands," imply competitors are no good. In comparative advertising over television, Nirma cakes do not become soggy whereas the "other" product does become soggy.

The Hidden Danger in Positioning: Once established in the minds of people, the association is such that it is very difficult to use the brand name, let alone positioning, to advantage. We have earlier cited the example of utterly butterly Amul. Here the association with butter is so well entrenched, AMUL name itself has become butter. To have such instant recall for Amul Icecream (where the positioning is "Taste of India.") or chocolate or cheese would be very difficult.

Creative Strategy—Implementation

Fig. 10.5: Red Tape uses sex appeal to sell shoes

Fig. 10.6: HIDESIGN—another example using sex to sell

An advertising appeal is used to make consumers aware of their needs and how the brand meets their needs. Advertising appeal is used to attract attention of consumers influence and motivate them in favour of a particular brand. Through the appeal the advertiser tries to excite the consumer, move him to buy a brand.

Advertising appeals are the basis for building effective advertising messages. There are several approaches for making appeal to the consumers. In the broadest sense we can classify appeals into two categories viz., rational appeals and emotional appeals.

Rational appeals are also identified as informational appeals. The appeals are primarily derived from tangible attributes of the brand. The tangible attributes can be product features which give comfort, convenience, economy, efficiency, performance. Rational approach can also include appeals relating to competitive advantage, popularity of the brand(largest selling brand),first in the market etc.

Emotional appeals relate to psychological and social needs of consumers. Many products do not connect well with consumers on rational appeals. For example, soft drink brands such as Coke and Pepsi are sold on fun appeals. Also appeals such as fear, hope motivate consumers faster to buy products such as insurance, cosmetics than rational appeals. These appeals are more directed to self than rational appeals which are directed toward the product or the competitor.

Fig. 10.7: Positioning by culture an example

Surrogate Advertising—Whom are you cheating?

Promotion of tobacco products and alcohol is banned in India like many other countries in the world. Despite the restriction, many marketers use the brand name of the banned products in promotion as if promoting a safe product like mineral water (Kingfisher), CDs(Bacardi), Playing cards (Royal Challenge) etc. This is called 'Surrogate Advertising'. Use of Kingfisher for UB airline, Wills for lifestyle garments—these surrogate advertising or mere brand extensions is a question to be pondered upon.

Humour—Sex—Fear

Most commercials and ads have one of these three themes:

Humour: The product is described in a humorous way so that you think it is funny, and will tell your friends, and the product will become known through word-of-mouth advertising.

The **Encyclopedia Britannica** defines humour as a form of communication in which a complex, mental stimulus illuminates, or amuses, or elicits the reflex of laughter. Many marketers use humour in advertising as a way of appealing to consumer's emotions. These positive emotions can potentially lead to cognitive processes that entice the consumer to purchase the related product. Doing it right means not only engaging the prospect but getting them to remember the product. However, that depends, among others, on social and psychological factors, how a person has been socialised may affect there judgment of humorous advertising. Humorous advertising can be found in variety of forms including TV, radio, print media and online.

Humour appeal has been used effectively by soft drink brands like Coca Cola, Pepsi Cola, confectionary brands like Chloromint, Polo etc. It is believed that humour helps hold viewer attention. Humour enhances message effectiveness by creating a positive mood. It increases the liking for the advertisement. Humour advertisements have a very short life because humour repeated becomes stale and viewer interest declines in a short time.

Humour is more used with products of low value. Generally, these products have little or no tangible benefit to the consumer. Products with high value are likely to risk credibility in using humour.

Sex: The product is described in a sexy way, to get you to pay attention, or the product is explained in a way that makes you think that if you use it, you will "get some". Using sex in ads is popular, but it can also be dangerous if it is considered too offensive, or if the audience is multi-cultural and will offend large segments of your target customer base so in most cases, companies combine Humour and Sex so they can get the sexy part of the message across, but use humour to cover up any offensive parts so people will laugh at it instead of getting "uptight" because it may have been offensive to some.

Gallup & Robinson, an advertising and marketing research firm, has reported that in more than 50 years of testing advertising effectiveness, it has found the use of the erotic to be a significantly above-average technique in communicating with the marketplace, "...although one of the more dangerous for the advertiser. Weighted down with taboos and volatile attitudes, sex is a Code Red advertising technique... handle with care... seller beware; all of which makes it even more intriguing." This research has led to the popular idea that "sex sells".

In contemporary mainstream consumer advertising (e.g., magazines, network and cable television), sex is present in promotional messages for a wide range of branded goods. Ads feature provocative images of well-defined women (and men) in revealing outfits and postures selling clothing, alcohol, beauty products and fragrances. Advertisers such as Calvin Klein, Victoria's Secret, and Pepsi use these images to cultivate a ubiquitous sex-tinged media presence. Also, sexual information is used to promote mainstream products not traditionally associated with sex. For example, the Dallas Opera recent reversal of declining ticket sales has been attributed to the marketing of the more lascivious parts of its performances.

Sex in advertising is the use of sexual or erotic imagery (also called "sex appeal") in advertising to draw interest to a particular product, for purpose of sale. A feature of sex in advertising is that the imagery used, such as that of a pretty woman, typically has no connection to the product being advertised. The purpose of the imagery is to attract the attention of the potential customer or user. The type of imagery that may be used is very broad, and would include nudity, cheesecake, and beefcake, even if it is often only suggestively sexual.

Images of pretty women often appear in ads even without connection to the product being sold. This provocatively clad woman lends "sex appeal" to a 1921 ad for tire valve caps Ivory Soap ads in World War I show sailors bathing on deck. Sex has been employed in advertising since the beginning of advertising. At the beginning, wood carvings and illustrations of attractive women (often unclothed from the waist up) adorned posters, signs, and ads for saloons, tonics, and tobacco. In several notable cases, sex in advertising has been claimed as the reason for increased consumer interest and sales. In 1885, W. Duke & Sons inserted trading cards into cigarette packs that featured sexually provocative starlets. Duke grew to become the leading cigarette brand by 1890 (Porter, 1971). Woodbury's Facial Soap, a woman's beauty bar, was almost discontinued in 1910. The soap's sales decline was reversed, however, with ads containing images of romantic couples and promises of love and intimacy for those using the brand (Account Histories, 1926). Jovan Musk Oil, introduced in 1971, was promoted with sexual entendre and descriptions of the fragrance's sexual attraction properties. As a result, Jovane, Inc.'s revenue grew from $1.5 million in 1971 to $77 million by 1978 (Sloan & Millman, 1979).

The use of sex in advertising can be highly overt or extremely subtle. It ranges from relatively explicit displays of sexual acts, to the use of basic cosmetics to enhance attractive features. Over the past two decades, the use of increasingly explicit sexual imagery in consumer-oriented print advertising has become almost commonplace. Sexuality is considered one of the most powerful tools of marketing and particularly advertising. Post-advertising sales response studies have shown it can be very effective for attracting immediate interest, holding that interest, and in the context of that interest, introducing a product that somehow correlates with that interest.

Fear: The product is described as being very important, and if you DO NOT use it, something bad may happen to you, you will not have fresh breath, or your car brakes will not stop you in the rain—fear is used to make you afraid if you do not buy the product. You have to be very careful using an ad based on fear because people do not like to feel they are being "threatened"—meaning if they do not spend hundreds of rupees to buy the product they will have an unhappy life —this can back-fire and cause anger against the product and make people discuss it negatively—which could create negative publicity for you to have to deal with.

Fear is an emotion evoked due to the threat which can cause harm to an individual. The harm can be physical or emotional. The customer buys the product to escape from this threat unhurt. Life Insurance has been sold in the past as a measure to provide a security in case of premature death of the wage earner. A cosmetic brand Fair and Lovely has been positioned as a solution to have fair complexion for girls and thereby prevent social rejection. A popular brand of disinfectant Lyzol is marketed to prevent infection of toddlers through invisible germs crawling on the floor.

Guilt Appeal (another form of fear appeal): Charity fund rising is often done by guilt appeals. The messages induce guilt feeling and consequently give rise to advocated social behaviour. Donation intentions can be increased by evoking feel good move. Helpage, SOS village, WorldVision are some of the NGOs which have used successfully guilt appeals to raise funds for charity.

Often working mothers are targeted by advertising messages to evoke guilt feeling. These mothers feel they are neglecting nourishment needs of their children and buy branded products like Bournvita, Horlicks, Complan etc.

Positioning—Appeals

Positoning in relation to competition: Also called comparative advertising, it is an approach where the competitor is directly or indirectly named and compared on one or more attributes. One of the problems with comparative advertising is the issue of credibility? Customers of the competing brand named are likely to be skeptical about the claim made by the advertised brand.

Horlicks pitched directly against Complan on both effectiveness of its content and price economy. Another long battle has been between Coca Cola and Pepsi through comparative advertising. However, there is inadequate data to confirm long-term benefits to these brands through comparative advertising.

Advertising standard council of India guideline on comparative advertising says that you cannot demean your competitor but factual comparison can be made. Advertisers should focus more on how they can position the benefits of their brand than showing how inferior the competing brand is.

Fig.10.8: Example of surrogate advertising

Fig. 10.9: Mufti-uses humour to promote its products

Advertising uses many feelings to form the basis for appeals to consumers. The feelings can be personal or social.Safety, security, fear, love, affection, happiness, joy, nostalgia, sentiment, excitement, arousal, sorrow, pride, achievement, self-esteem, actualisation, pleasure, ambition, comfort, are some of the personal feelings. Recognition, status, respect, involvement, embrassment, belonging, rejection, acceptance, approval, are some of the social feelings.

Fig.10.10: REAL positions itself against ordinary fruit juice

Emotional advertisements are used to create high recall of the brand. Emotional advertising also helps transform positive feelings which can be gained by the use of the brand. Emotional appeals are also used to influence consumer interpretation of their product usage experience.

Celebrity Advertising

Advertising uses brand endorsers to influence consumer buying. The attitude of consumers towards a brand is no doubt shaped by internalized attributes including motivation, personality, learning process, perception etc. However, between the attitude and the final behaviour of buying many products endorsers appear to have a great influence.

Advertising uses three types of endorsers. They are professionals (or experts), celebrity, and ordinary consumers-slice of life advertising.

Some of the celebrity endorsers are Amitabh Bachchan for Cadbury, ICICI, Navratna Oil; Sharukh Khan for Santro, Lux; Shewag and Sachin Tendulkar for Boost; Aishwarya Rai for Nakshatra; Sania Mirza for Sony Erricsson.

Slice of life or consumer centric advertising used products which are typically used in the house. Harpic, Surf, Close Up are some of the examples of consumers being used as endorsers.

Generally, products of conspicuous consumption use celebrity endorser. Technical products tend to use expert endorsers. Low-value products use slice of life mode of advertising.

Transformation advertising is used to achieve this. Transformation advertising is defined as one which creates a unique association of the brand with the experience of using the brand with a unique set of psychological characteristics which cannot be associated with any other brand. Transformation advertising makes the experience of the product richer, more exciting more enjoyable. The brand experience is tightly knitted with the experience with the advertisement. Master card advertising campaign is created in such a way that the experience of spending money is closely linked with the brand through series of creative advertisements.

Fig. 10.11: Aishwarya Rai modelling for Nakshatra

Fig. 10.12: Hema and daughters ask you to buy Kent Water Purifiers

Fig.10.13: Another good example of Celebrity Endorsement in Advertising

When Volkswagon launched a plush large car of high quality, people were so accustomed to associate the name with the 'small' car, there was no market for the new car!

Big Idea

The exercise of positioning must lead to a big idea. This is indeed difficult. As David Ogilvy, one of the greatest said, "It's not too difficult to decide on how to produce the product. Any intelligent person can do it. But it takes a genius to create a big idea based on positioning." This is part of "Creatives" in the next few pages.

Summary

Positioning is the most important step in strategic marketing after segmentation and targeting. Positioning is the art of identifying a segment of the market to which the brand gets attached. Positioning uses approaches like positioning by attributes, positioning by use, positioning by application.

Advertising uses several creative strategies to communicate the message of a brand. Different appeals can be used to transfer a brand message. Appeals can be either rational appeals or emotional appeals. Rational appeals use tangible attributes of the product/ brand like price, quality, packaging, colour, taste, size, etc. Emotional appeals satisfy the psychological needs while making a purchase decision. Emotional appeals commonly used are sex, humour, fear and guilt.

Surrogate advertising uses promotion of products which normally is now legally allowed by associating and promoting same brand for products which are not prime target for marketing.

Advertising uses celebrities for promoting brands. However, there are risks associated in using celebrities e.g., Tiger Woods or Salman Khan.

Keywords

- Catchy slogan
- Mid-strength strategies
- Pre-emptive strategies
- Unique selling proposition
- Attribute
- Consumer orientation
- Positioning by attribute
- Positioning by product usage
- Positioning in relation to compotator
- Sex appeal
- Fear appeal
- Surrogate advertising
- Weak strategies
- Strong strategies
- Generic Strategies
- Positioning
- Benefits
- Commercial orientation
- Positioning by application
- Positioning by product class
- Surrogate advertising
- Humour appeal
- Guilt appeal

Discussion Question

1. 'Positioning is a key to effective communication'. Discuss.

11

Media Planning

11

Media Planning

Media

The dictionary meaning of media is "means by which something is communicated."

Media Guru Marshal McLuhan provided great insights into media in his books **Understanding Media** and **The Medium is the Message**.

McLuhan has also divided Media as "Hot" or "Cold." Hot media do not leave much to be filled by audience and is low in audience participation. On the other hand, Cold media gives so little that filling in is to be done by the audience who therefore participate a great deal.

What media are available to the marketing communications exercises?

The first classification is mass media and other media.

The second is organised media and unorganised media.

The third is modern and traditional media.

All three are terminologies and mean the same thing: two types of media—mass/organised/modern media refer to print, television, radio and to some extent cinema and outdoor.

Other unorganised/traditional media refer to such media as rural vans, house-to-house demonstrations, distribution of literature, wall paintings, drum beaters, etc.

A rough list of media would be as follows:

Print	Newspapers—Dailies (morning or evening, regular size or tabloid size) National, State, District, even local. General News, Financial/Economics etc. Magazines: Weeklies, Fortnightlies, Monthlies. General interest, Political, Economic, Fashion, Women's Health, Special interest such as Sports, Racing, Autos etc. Information Technology, Health and so on. Quarterlies, Half Yearlies, Annuals, Directories, Yellow Pages etc.
Television	All the channels in every possible language/ Sports, Religion/Fashion, Nature, Travel, News, Weather and so on.
Radio	National, State, FM—covering a variety of subjects and/or music only/and talk shows too.
Outdoor	Hoardings, Banners, Wall Paintings, Lamp Posts, Bus Shelters, Neon Signs, Lighted Signs, etc.
Transport	Railway carriages, buses, trams, autorickshaws, hired vehicles etc.
Cinema	Theatres where short films/slides etc., are screened
Window Display	Shop/Hotel etc., windows

Besides these, there are: Sponsored events, Event management, and several other media.

Expos	Exhibitions, Fairs, Melas.
Rural	Vans, stenciling on walls, participation in shandi markets.
Traditional	Street Theatre, Drum Beaters , Harikathas etc.
Internal Media	Direct mailing, e-mailing, Fax, SMS, Bulletins, Presentations, etc.

The above list is only illustrative and not a complete list.

Fig. 11.1: Hoarding—A popular outdoor medium

Media and Marketing Communications

We need to recall how newspapers—a long time ago—"recognised" advertising agencies and allowed 15% commission and also how advertising agencies developed. Then, newspapers were mainly "local" and did not carry advertisements for a long time.

The mission of newspapers or for that matter any medium is to provide news, views, educate, entertain. There are, however, purely advertising media too like tenders today, real estate and so on.

When advertising developed, this became a source of revenue for media and helped media subsidise their costs. For example, a newspaper can never be sold for as low as Rs. 3 (with 20 odd pages). It would cost some Rs.7 or more. Likewise, it will not be possible to offer free airing of TV and radio programmes but for advertising revenue.

Most media carry the statement that they do not take responsibility for what is advertised.

It is the advertiser who gains by exposing his message to the audience of the media concerned.

With growing competition and in a situation where without advertising revenue a medium cannot exist, media do research and provide the advertiser with a profile of their audience apart from the geographical coverage, etc.

Media Strategy

The media reach differs from state to state. For example, AP and Tamil Nadu together will account for over 50% of the cinema houses in India—one theatre per 20,000 or so population while in Bihar it will be just a few and one theatre for 3 lakh population. Within states, some districts are poor in media reach (e.g., Northern Karnataka). While language media has better reach all over India. In Bangalore (Bengaluru), it is the English print media that has more coverage. These aspects need to be understood since professionals do not go into great details.

What media should be used? This will be a match of the audience profile of media and the profile of the target audience. What should be the media mix? This will depend on the budget and task. Should special positions be used? The strategy will answer these and other questions and these will relate to the time frames and tasks set by the marketing communications objective.

Media Planning

For the advertiser, the media for marketing would include the sales force, distribution network, the brand, the package, display on the dealers' shelves and also sales promotion, public relations and mass media advertising. He allocates his budget resources in such a way that he gets the best returns on his spend. At the same time, he needs to coordinate the efforts so that the combined impact exceeds his targets in terms of tasks accomplished, sales achieved, market share improved etc.

Some of these he controls. However, when it comes to mass media, the Media Planner in the advertising agency (some advertisers have their own planners too) is the person who does the planning. He first sets the media objectives.

Media Objectives

(i) Geographical areas to be covered.

(ii) Target audience: age group, sex, educational level, occupation, etc.

(iii) Lifestyle.

(iv) Seasonality.

(v) Family or individual (divorcees in the US are also a group).

(vi) Strategy.

(vii) Time frame for the campaign or would it be sustained over successive years.

(viii) Extra efforts required in specific terms: for example, some markets would need larger space/more frequency and other efforts to supplement the effort.

The media planner is a well-informed expert who is up to the minute on the media scene, shifts, new developments etc. The ground rule he follows is, "have no preconceived notion" of what media should be employed when confronted with a particular situation/problem. The reason being that we are in a state of change all the time and no two situations or time frames are the same. He has to look at media strategy as a business proposition, one that works and meets the tasks. He does not look at the job as one of just advertising but as spending wisely in order to get results.

He utilises the latest and updated data on media and his task is to prepare a media plan. This should be cost effective and the media mix should impact by complementing and by reinforcing the message. The data he uses includes the claims of media as also research studies by independent and authoritative sources. The media plan takes into account the market, the task, the time frame, etc., as related to the target consumer. He looks at wastage factors, size of advertisements/length of commercials, positions—if it is print advertising, will it be a solus (fixed) position, top of the page, right hand side or left, which page, on what days of the week or the weekend and so on.

He has to strategically consider and evaluate media alternatives, innovations, the frequency for maximum impact without throwing money away.

Like the creative personnel, the media strategist and the media planner are briefed as early on as possible all aspects of the client's problem and plans. He is fully aware of the marketing plans, the competition, the objectives, the strategies (including sales promotion inputs/public relations efforts etc.) and sometimes even the route plans of sales personnel. He has to work the best plan within the budget. He should also be prepared for tactical changes in the plan, for revisions etc.

The media planner decides on the main media, supplementary/ reminder media (the character of some media are taken into account: for example, outdoor or radio can do the job of reminding better.) He decides how much weightage to be given to which media and programme.

Media Selection

A good media planner does a highly "creative" function. He would reject unviable and ineffective media, from the viewpoint of the objectives first. Then he would look at the reach factors, comparative merits and demerits, duplicate readership/viewership factors, wasted exposures etc., and concentrate on "value for money."

He would also be practical. For the same product for two different situations, he might recommend two different sets of media. For example, for a food or convenience product for regular promotion the media mix he suggests could be television and magazines as primary media and radio as the reminder media. For the same product, when there is a special offer or promotion, he might—for reasons of efficacy alone—restrict his recommendation to daily newspapers, outdoor, local television, cinema slide and radio.

The media planner would be aware of the restrictions on products/ claims imposed by various media codes.

Note: Some of the readily available media data sources include:

(i) INFA Annual

(ii) Audit Bureau of Circulations

(iii) Indian Newspaper Society Handbook

(iv) National Readership Survey

(v) Audience surveys of **Doordarshan and Akashvani**

(vi) UP-Market studies/TV ratings etc., by independent sources

(vii) Case studies/papers presented in seminars/workshops

(viii) Published research in advertising/marketing magazines

(ix) Claims/Data by media

(x) Others

Testing Effectiveness of Advertising

There are many studies on positions used for advertising—the first or last commercial in a TV programme, right hand side in a magazine advertisement, a solus(fixed) position in newspapers and so on. In addition, advertisers use research and tests to find out the effectiveness of their advertising—first pre-testing them and later on, during and after campaign. Good consumer research organisations just as market research organisations do research in their special areas of research.

Can a reminder medium be used as the main medium? In certain circumstances yes. If it is a seasonal product, like during very hot season a soft drink uses outdoor as the main medium supplemented by point of sale and display in the dealer's outlets. In North India, during the 1960s, trucks were owner-driven and these owners were not literate. The only medium used was hoardings on highways, placed close to the check posts and/or **dhabas**.

The use of media depends on knowledge and application of that knowledge.

Keywords

- Media planning
- Other media
- Mudern media
- Event management
- Solus position
- Channel of delivery
- Organised media
- Traditional media e-mailing
- Main media
- Mass media
- Unorganised media
- Sponsored events
- Tattoo
- Supplementary/ Reminder media

12

Direct Marketing

12

Direct Marketing

The term direct marketing is believed to be first used in 1967 in a speech by Lester Wunderman, who pioneered direct marketing with brands such as American Express and Columbia Records.The term junk mail is used to describe unsolicited mail. The term Spam meaning unsolicited commercial e–mail can be traced back to 1973.The practice of mail order selling began in the US in 1867.

Increasing marketing costs, channels distancing the customer from the marketer, increasing competition, marketing of new concepts are some of the reasons for the growth of direct marketing in India. Direct marketing tools are more frequently used by companies to promote products as diverse as cosmetics to aircraft.

In the dictionary of marketing terms, direct marketing is defined as the sum total of all activities by which the marketer in effecting the exchange of products, uses one or more media to a target audience for the purpose of creating a response by phone, mail, Internet or personal visit from a sales person. The marketer may use personal selling, mail, phone, TV etc., for this purpose.

Direct marketing is a system through which companies try to evoke responses from prospects without use of intermediary channels. The interface between the marketer and the customer totally eliminates presence of channel members such as distributors, wholesalers, retailers etc.

Direct marketing can be done in combination with other components of promotion mix.

Direct marketing is a collection of techniques that enable organisations to market products directly to customers

(Business to customer or B to C). It is a proactive approach to marketing that takes the products to customers without the use of intermediaries. It is a form of "non-shop" shopping referred to as one to one marketing. Direct marketing tends to target specific individuals or households. The firm is eliminating the use of intermediaries and selling directly to customers. This has implication for both channel and logistical decision.

There are two main features of direct marketing. Firstly, it attempts to send messages directly to customers (direct mail, e-mail, telephone) usually unsolicited. Secondly, it tries to evoke a direct response from the customers (it attempts to make the customer act).

Attributes of Direct Marketing

Direct marketing has following distinct advantages over other methods of promotion.

Focus: A well—segmented group of prospects is targeted to direct the message.

Personalisation: The message is directed towards an individual.

Immediacy: It tries to evoke response immediately.

Measurability: It is possible to measure responses for each communication.

Channels of Direct Marketing

Direct Mails: This is the most common form of direct mail. Advertisers send conventional paper mail to customers through post by using a list of mailing address. The word junk mail is used to describe such unsolicited mail.

Mail includes advertising circulars, catalogues, free trial CDs, credit card applications, request for contributions, trial samples delivered to customers. Bulk mailing is a popular method of promotion for financial services, travel and tourism industries, electronic home entertainment products etc.

In many developed countries bulk mailing forms significant amount of total volume of mail. Bulk mail rates are much lower than normal individual mail rate.

Direct mail uses database marketing. Advertisers refine their data base by selecting target segment thus improving the focus of marketing efforts. For example, a person who has shown interest in photography may receive mailers for products related to photography.

Telemarketing: The second most popular form of direct marketing is telemarketing. In this method marketers contact prospects through telephone. The unpopularity of unsolicited calls has resulted in legislation by government to protect privacy of telephone users.

e-mail marketing: This is the third type of direct marketing which is gaining popularity with increased use of Internet in India. Unsolicited mail called 'spam' is of a major concern. e-mail service providers offer e-mail filters to eliminates spasm.

Door to through leaflets: Door marketing through Leaflet distribution services are widely used by fast food outlets, supermarkets, and other service providers like beauty saloons, libraries, to capture the neighbourhood markets. This method is used to target areas, and very inexpensive as compared to direct mail. No mailing cost is involved in this method.

Television marketing: Direct marketing on TV has two forms. Long form using half to one hour explaining in detail the product. Short form of 30 seconds to 60 seconds asking customers for immediate response. Many health products use the first format.

Direct selling: Direct selling is done through personal selling when a sales person calls on a prospect to sell a product. Tuepperware, Amway use parties for selling.

Integrated campaign

Marketers use a mix of channels of direct marketing campaign. It is not unusual for a large campaign to combine direct mail, telemarketing, radio and TV as well as new channels like e-mail, social networking etc.

Advantages of Direct Marketing

The advantages of direct marketing are:

(i) **Focused approach:** Marketers can identify specific segments by looking at demographic data like age, sex and education. Then design the appropriate message and channel and suit the segment.

(ii) **Reduce wastage:** Through selecting the right target group the message is directed to the hot prospects and prevent wastage of efforts. For example, a hoarding attracts many viewers of whom several may have no interest in buying the product.

(iii) **Frequency:** Because of its low cost as compared to other promotional tools frequency can be increased to gain impact and increase effectiveness.

(iv) **Immediate and flexible:** The response from direct marketing is immediate. It also provides flexibility in creativity. Direct marketing are used to send CDs on products to be marketed.

(v) **Lead time:** Relatively a direct marketing campaign can be put together in a short time. Buying space/time in media on a casual basis can bring economy in spending.

(vi) **Personalisation:** Insurance buyers are congratulated on their decision to buy insurance through personalised mail.

(vii) **Measuring effectiveness:** Effectiveness of promotion can be easily measured in direct marketing. Feedback is immediate and likely to be accurate.

Disadvantage of Direct Marketing

The disadvantage of direct marketing is:

(i) Direct marketing is seen as nuisance by many customers. Junk mail and spam are ignored. Telemarketing by firms is seen as invasion of privacy. These factors may negatively impact the brand image.

Fig. 12.1: Filmfare takes the route of direct marketing to sell subscription

Direct marketing is widely used by companies in India. Some of the applications are:

(a) Marketing of credit cards by HSBC, Citibank etc.

(b) Marketing of restaurant services: Oberoi, Grand Ashok.

(c) Marketing of resorts: Sterling, RCI.

(d) Marketing of durables: Eureka Forbes.

(e) Marketing of magazines: **Readers Digest**.

(f) Marketing of consumer products through catalogue:Burlington.

(g) Marketing of mobile services: Spice.

(h) Promotion of conferences and workshops

Direct marketing is based on one to one marketing strategy. Its effectiveness largely depends on the database. Some of the important sources of databases are following:

(a) Census report.

(b) Telephone directory.

(c) Postal pin codes.

(d) Credit card holders' name list.

(e) Members of a club.

(f) Research Agencies.

However, access to databases is now being legally restricted to provide privacy to individuals.

Direct Marketing can be done through:

(a) Advertising in print or broadcasting media.

(b) Personal selling.

(c) Marketing on Internet.

(d) Telephone marketing.

(e) TeleSky.

Return of the DM

In spite of several associations coming out in favour of direct marketing. It lacks credibility due to perception people have about it. Customer fear database leak like many of the support services direct marketing has a low profile compared to advertising agencies.

However,many in the industry believe that for certain category of products direct marketing agency is more relevant than advertising agency. It appears that direct marketing takes the lead is effective for less established brands.

Several consumer products manufacturers have taken the route of direct marketing through multilevel marketing. Amway, Tupperware, Swadeshi, are some of the successful MLMs in India.

Summary

Direct Marketing is a system through which companies try to evoke responses from prospects without use of intermediary channels. Interface between the marketer and the customer totally eliminates presence of channel members like distributors, wholesalers, retailers etc.

Direct marketing is a versatile promotional tool in the hands of marketers. It can be used singularly or combined with other promotional tools of marketing. It offers great advantages in cost and also works as a focused promotion with minimum wastages.

Advantages of direct marketing include segmentation, personalisation, increased frequency of communication, flexibility in creativity and easy measurement of effectiveness.

Some of the disadvantages of direct marketing are negative image due to customer perception. The general public believes direct marketing invades the privacy of individuals. Success of direct marketing largely depends on database. Effectiveness of direct marketing can be diluted due to defective database.

Direct marketing is being used not only for industrial products but also for marketing consumer products such as cosmetics, soap etc.

Keywords

- Direct Marketing
- Personalisation
- Telemarketing
- Database
- Mailing list

Discussion Questions

1. Discuss various forms of direct marketing.
2. Explain role of direct marketing in strengthening other promotional tools.

13

Sales Promotion

13

Sales Promotion

In the US, where the discipline of marketing was born, if one goes out shopping, one will never be able to find the "real" price of any product. There is always a kind of sale going on—in every outlet, be it for automobiles or for day-to-day consumer products. The exception would probably be shops like Costco or Sams, which sell, always for cash/personal cheques, bulk quantities to members at what can be termed Cost price + minimum profit. In India, Metro shops are good examples.

The reason is not difficult to discover. Competition has intensified, there are more products and outlets need to ensure faster turnover and would not wish to stock items that stay on shelves for long. Space costs money, employees cost money and returns must be as quick as possible. Unless outlets keep the goods moving, manufacturers would not be able to keep up levels of production.

In our own country, on a dealer's shelves, there are more products than ever before. In 1990, a medium sized outlet had 2,500 or less stock units. By 1995, this rose to 5,000 and by 2000 to over 8,500 items. Apart from totally new products (like the clog remover in drains like Draino and other products), there have been more versions of the same product. In the 1960s, we had just one shampoo for the hair. Today, we have dandruff preventing shampoos, shampoos for dry hair and so on, and also conditioners. Earlier we had one size of pack, today we have many, including sachets. Grocery items such as wheat and sugar and pulses are now available packed. All these compete for shelf space. Even chemists have added lines other than pharmaceutical.

The answer: Find ways of attracting customers and sell them as many goods as possible. The central problem of marketing management is that of bringing about buying action—by consumers. To do this, offer incentives. Offering incentives, in short, is sales promotion. Sales promotion by itself cannot build brands and relationship as other means of marketing communications, spearheaded by advertising do. Yet, sales promotion is today a vital and growing component of marketing communications. Sales promotion activities are by and large done through the field force and distribution outlets, although direct promotion is also done.

Through sales promotion, advertisers INDUCE or PUSH sales. Promotion is defined by Haugh as:

"A promotion is a direct inducement that offers an extra value incentive to the sales force/distributor/the ultimate consumer—with the primary objective of creating an immediate sale."

Obviously, sales promotion, although it uses advertising, differs from regular advertising. Regular advertising, by definition, has a task to perform and about this, we have studied earlier. Now, the differences between sales promotion and advertising can be stated as follows:

Advertising	Sales Promotion
Appeals to the heart.	Appeals to the purse.
AttemptstocreatePULL(demandby customers).	Attempts to create PUSH to consumers.
Essentially,communicationthrough mass media.	Essentially uses sales force/ distributionsystem,whichareunder company's control.
Alsoaimsatnon–targetandfuture audience.	Aimsattargetaudienceandfortrial purchaselevels/thebargainhunting audience.
Aimsatmaximumcoverageatleast cost.	Inducespurchasesatextracosttothe company.

Sales promotion has also been defined as "all marketing efforts other than personal selling/advertising/publicity, that enhance dealer effectiveness/consumer buying.

Objectives of Sales Promotion

Gain/Hasten trial among non-users of the brand:

(i) Help introduce an improved version or a line extension.

(ii) Increase repeat/multiple purchase by current users.

(iii) Expand product usage.

(iv) Defend market against threat from (or counter) competition/ powerful new entrant.

(v) Reinforce current "position" and image—built by advertising.

(vi) Soften impact of a price increase.

(vii) Gain 'cross item' trial within a line of products (among say four different flavours to be added to a food item when only one is popular).

(viii) Synergically enhance the result of another promotion device (e.g., recipe booklet against coupons for a cooking oil).

(ix) Increase distribution in a given area/during the introductory stage/as a sales drive.

(x) Support and increase retail trade efforts. Promotions fetch the dealers faster turnover.

(xi) Ensure trade offtake during festive seasons: e.g., it is customary in India to offer discounts on clothing during Diwali/Pongal/New Year etc., or during off season (fans during cold months).

(xii) Strategic reasons—focus attention away from established position so as to introduce a new strategy or position later.

(xiii) Liquidate stocks of current pack/model paving the way for a new introduction.

(xiv) Reward the existing users.

(xv) Sell more during off season.

(xvi) Shot in the arm to slow selling items.

(xvii) Help sales staff achieve targets.

Steps for Undertaking Sales Promotion

The steps for undertaking sales promotion are as follows:

(i) Thorough knowledge about consumers. Who buys what or who ought to buy or who is the decision maker. Trends, Distribution systems/factors. Strategy followed by existing brands.

(ii) Communications objectives include the basic sales ideas for each group. Specifically, how the company wishes to change attitudes towards its product and how it wishes to increase knowledge of each group for this.

(iii) Evolve a sales promotion plan for each group. Select the most effective form for each and the relevant cost effective media mix/best coverage.

(iv) Work out a PERT chart.

(v) Estimate costs.

(vi) Coordinate/Dovetail the programme into a coherent, cohesive campaign.

(vii) Work out the strategy for repeated efforts, cycles for visits to dealers/repeat advertising etc.

(viii) Work out a time frame and stick to it.

In Sales Promotion, TIME is money—spent and or earned.

The Company Sales Force

The inducement to the sales personnel could be in diverse ways. One of the commonest is a commission on sales based on a tier system. Another is a surprise gift, which may be a much larger sum than a commission. Yet another is a Star system, where the best achievers get incentives. Besides, these there are paid family foreign trips, vehicles as gifts, gold and the like.

There is also a points system, which covers everyone in the sales team. Points are awarded at regular intervals and the individual is free to convert these points at any point into cash/gifts.

Shares in the company are also given as a sign of recognition.

Distributors

This term includes retail outlets/agents etc., and the incentives given depend on the task. For example, certain products such as fans, air conditioners etc., have less demand in cold weather and this is termed as 'off season'. In order to keep production at viable levels, the company offers extra commissions. These, in addition to giving more income, also cover cost of space, interest etc.

For some products like cement, there are outlets that sell more than one brand. Here, the incentives are to (a) take extra stocks and (b) try and reduce the influence of the competition.

In general, however, retail outlets are pampered in many ways:

(i) For a new/existing product (if promotion is done), attractive discount in the invoice.

(ii) Parcel offer: for ordering/buying a mix of existing and new products.

(iii) Pay for a dozen, get three pieces extra.

(iv) Voucher bonuses: the vouchers are redeemed for cash/kind/ against future orders.

(v) Display allowances in cash.

(vi) Stock up bonus: for carrying a minimum stock all the time.

(vii) Sales contests.

(viii) Scratch and win schemes, with a minimum gift assured.

(ix) Paid holidays for the family and more.

Consumer Promotions

Consumer promotions mean quick turnover for the trade too and therefore more common in today's environment. In recent times, there have been innovations too. The many consumer offers include:

(i) Free – 20% extra (more of the product in a slightly larger pack).

(ii) Buy one take one free.

(iii) Banded offer: Buy this, take another product.

(iv) Buy a plane ticket (in Executive Class) take your companion for free.

(v) For automobiles: Free insurance/gold articles etc.

(vi) Consumer contests.

(vii) Slogan contests.

(viii) SMS your choice: (common in TV programmes—for huge prize offers, but here, the audience does not realise that several crores of revenue accrues to the advertiser).

Fig. 13.1: Filmfare conducts a consumer contest

(ix) Every week a winner of educational scholarship worth Rs. 5 lakh (or more), in order to really step up sales.

(x) Free gift with each purchase.

(xi) Collect coupons (inside the pack) and for so and so number exchange for a dictionary and things like that.

(xii) An opportunity to have dinner with (an icon).

(xiii) Free holiday for two – all expenses paid.

(xiv) Scratch and win one of the many gifts.

(xv) Price off – only till ....

(xvi) Exchange your old (whatever) for the new (whatever) at only Rs... .

There are scores of variations and one comes across newer versions/innovations in consumer promotion.

Innovations: Apart from novel schemes, new habits get promoted by the marketing organisations. Whoever heard of Akshayathithi in the 1980s and early 1990s? Suddenly, the idea of buying gold on that 'auspicious' day was promoted and has caught on resulting in increasing demand for this yellow metal year by year. Such innovations too belong to the area of consumer promotion.

As we saw earlier, the marketplace is becoming more and more crowded and consumer promotion has become a key ingredient for getting priority in the minds of people for a product class/product. The emergence of malls, super bazaars, chain stores and self-service outlets where products are displayed makes promotion an imperative—for impulse buying and also attracting to the specific brand.

This obviously means that consumer behaviour needs to be influenced/shaped. Just fantasise a situation when every male had a beard. First came the barbers, then the same razors used by the barber for self-shaving; these were sharpened on leather belts or stone and the adventurous person who shaved nicked his chin. Then it became a fashion, set by obviously an icon—maybe the Emperor himself—to shave regularly. Competition/Product developments took place (they are taking place even now), leading to blades and now to systems. We do see promotions for the new systems on the television. Schemes and ploys to get customers flow into shops have resulted in the creation of "Retail Advertising" and ad agencies have special personnel to develop this facet.

When aspects like memory, hierarchy etc., were studied, it was understood that several barriers had to be overcome to make the first (initial) sale. Through marketing communications, we draw the attention of people, make them aware; take interest and then buy the product. To make them continue to buy until it becomes a habit is equally complex. Promotions do help in an increasingly competitive/ crowded market.

Through promotions, we can (**a**) gain entry and trial through the incentive, (**b**) offer something more for a repeat purchase in the case of consumer perishables (e.g., a coupon collection scheme or a price off on producing empty pack etc.) (**c**) try variations of 1 and 2, and finally (**d**) reach the final stage where the consumer buys our product because of its PERFORMANCE and not because of the incentive.

The last stage is critical. Once incentives are withdrawn, a consumer may switch to another brand that offers the advantage. This implies that care should be taken to guard the differential in quality/image in the minds of buyers all the time. This is where the phrase, "MANAGING CONSUMER BEHAVIOUR" is tested. The product if it were to protect its market share and leadership, needs to always STAND OUT. Otherwise, the behaviour pattern would be mismanaged and vitiated.

Sales promotion works best when consumers are not keen to make the best brand choice or use a brand class where brands do not have much of a product differential. Consumer behaviour theories are many but a good advertiser would research and this would reveal statements like, "I liked the brand, the name and pack appealed to me and I am quite satisfied." Or, one like, "I liked the free gift, which will be very useful to me." When the statement is the latter one, the marketing communicator can easily infer that his product does not STAND OUT. What the research would reveal is that the consumer loyalty has not been established at all.

New Brands

It would make sense to undertake promotion for a new product, even sampling, in order to expedite trial and an introductory price off or gift would perhaps gain customers.

This will not be necessary if the product concept itself is totally new and it performs what it promises. A good example would be the drain clog cleaner. This product gained immediate acceptance.

Only the distribution network may need promotion besides regular advertising.

For "me too" products, it is unlikely that a customer would shift from his trusted brand. He would feel it a risk to try the new brand in the absence of any justifiable reason. Therefore, the new brand must have some plausible differentiation. Like Promise toothpaste claimed "clove" oil content. For any consumer, even to consider a new brand, there needs to be one or two new and attractive/ compelling features.

The question arises, "Are promotions profitable?" Until a few years ago, the experience was, as a one-time or occasional incentive, this could be profitable but in the long run it would add costs (and when competition offers more incentives, the leader is also compelled to up the ante) and weaken the competitive differential. However, today the scene is different and the pricing structure (a) itself takes care of maintaining the product differential and (b) by subtle and indirect methods, offers incentives. This is why, in the advanced US, one can never be sure of the actual price of a product. There is a totally new outlook on the use of promotions as a weapon.

Promotions can be related to user segments as follows:

Segment	Characteristics	Value of promotion to the Advertiser for this segment
Loyal	Donotneed/useincentives	Never profitable
Loyal	Do go for deals	Never profitable
Loyal	Will switch brands	Occasionallyprofitable,depends on market share
Loyal	Willswitchforbetterdeals	Occasionallyprofitable,depends on market share
Switchers	Do not need/use deals	Never profitable
Switchers	Use deals	Occasionallyprofitabledependson market share
Switchers	Use deal to stock up	Occasionallyprofitabledependson market share
No loyalty	Buy only on deals	Always profitable unless sold at loss
No loyalty	Will also stock up	Always profitable unless sold at loss

The present situation in the marketplace has placed great emphasis on Relationship Marketing where the mission is to build loyal customers for life and make such customers the advocates (powerful media)/brand ambassadors.

Here it must be re-emphasized that promotion cannot

(a) Build a consumer franchise

(b) Overcome a product deficiency

(c) Overcome (other) marketing errors

Caution: Sales promotion can become a powerful drug to the marketing person responsible for increasing sales—because of the instant, immediate acceleration in sales. This is short term. If the advertiser falls for this drug and gets addicted, the dosage of sales promotion will increase along with cost escalation and change in consumer behaviour. This exercise will make the consumer "incentive oriented" rather than becoming a loyal customer.

Thus, sales promotion, even in the current context, needs to be used with caution, judiciously and not abused. The communications should reinforce the positioning of the product in the minds of the consumer.

Fig.13.2: Price discount as a tool of sales promotion

Summary

Sales promotion is a powerful tool used by marketers to induce immediate sales/purchases of their brand. Sales promotion can be directed to the consumer, trade or the sales staff of the company. Sales promotions can be in the form of price discounts, contests, gifts, samples, offers etc.

Sales promotion should be selectively used as an occasional shot to accelerate sales or to liquidate the slow moving stocks. Making sales promotion as a permanent feature would result in damage to the brand image.

The choice of sales promotion used will depend on the nature of the product for example, in general samples could be effective in fast moving consumer goods where as demonstration is good for consumer durables such as TV, Washing Machines etc.

Keywords

- Sales Promotion
- Inducement
- Points system
- Stock of bonus
- Product differential
- Consumer franchise

Discussion Question

1. 'Sales promotion is an indirect method of price reduction.' Do you agree with this?

14

Publicity and Public Relations

14

Publicity and Public Relations

Public Relations

Public relations and publicity are secret weapons of integrated marketing communication. Public relations is a critical component of integrated marketing. Public relation improves effectiveness of integrated marketing communications, while advertising is an important tool in communication, public relations enables improved credibility of advertising. Public relations acts as a glue in holding together other elements of communication used in marketing.

The relationship between public relations and marketing is growing stronger as marketers recognise the importance of building relationship between the brand and the consumer. Brand building is a long process and takes help of public relations in this process.

Public relations and publicity helps introducing new products before the advertising campaign begins. Public relations and publicity use celebrities for launching new products. Advertorials can help in telling a story about the brand being launched. Advertorials play a very important role particularly in products which have breakthrough innovations.

There are several ways of looking at Public Relations. One as good manners; another as developing Goodwill. These apart, our concern is professional public relations. Under the nomenclature "Public Relations," Ivy Lee launched his Consultancy in the US in 1903. This has grown into a management discipline worldwide and is concerned with the image of a company/organisation/ Government etc., and its products/services. There are several worldwide and Indian Public Relations

Consultancies in our country whose services are used widely by organisations.

The Institute of Public Relations, whose definition is most accepted, describes this discipline as "The deliberate, planned and sustained effort to establish and maintain mutual understanding between the organisation and its publics."

Every organisation has a philosophy that is manifest in its 'Mission and Vision' statements. It is within this parameter that all disciplines function and follows a work ethic. As such, the Marketing discipline and therefore Marketing Communications too would need to work within the framework of a Corporate PR policy. Public Relations is applied to every activity of the organisation be it Finance, HR, Industry, Government liaison or whatever.

At the Corporate level, product launches, new versions, new packaging etc., are made known through launch conferences (where the Public Relations head organises these). In addition, to popularising the product, celebrity endorsements are obtained and icons are featured to promote.

When there is an adverse report about the company or the product (as it happened with an aerated soft drink company whose product was found below world standards), the Public Relations experts first straighten out the problem and get over the damage done—set the course once again on the growth path/reinforce a positive image.

In Marketing Communications, the Publics or the Audience segments are the Sales Force, the Distribution Network and the Target (consumer) audience. In every component of Marketing and Marketing activities, Public Relations is present.

One area that is active in the Marketing side consists of Bouquets and Brickbats. Bouquets are letters of appreciation and brickbats are complaints. A good organisation will circulate the bouquets to all, including sometimes, to the media. It will also attend to complaints (brickbats) very quickly and ensure that shortcomings are overcome so that there is no repetition of the problem.

Sales Force

Nowadays, it is common to see icons (sports personalities, beauty queens and the like) named Brand Ambassadors. However, the **de facto** Brand ambassadors are the sales people. They are the 'FACE' of the organisation to the outside world. They deal with others in the office/with the trade/with the public. Their Public Relations begins with Good Manners. In this they need to behave as dignified ambassadors, when calling on the trade. There is nothing sweeter than recognition of a person by his name. If the ambassador would only greet the retailer by his name—adding whatever he is normally called, such as Mister or **Dadha, Bhaiya** or **Annachi** or whatever. Add the good manners to knowledge and the art of selling. These skills help the person to overcome blocks, create lasting goodwill and helps him and thereby the organisation succeed.

The organisation ensures two-way communication with the sales force—at work situations through interactions, reports, advice and help and the like. These are supplemented with Sales Bulletins, presentations and other tools that would improve the caliber of the field staff.

Success stories are shared and also spoken about in relevant forums. Media carry stories too. A sales person helping out during a disaster (like Tsunami), donating blood at a critical moment etc., is appreciated by the organisation, which also makes it known (to its advantage too) in the media. Likewise, a sports person's (on the rolls of the organisation) achievements are also recognised by the organisation/media.

The organisation undertakes what is called Internal Public Relations exercises with the employees. Marketing people are exposed to other disciplines, regular training sessions are organised, socialising/get-togethers ensure interaction between different disciplines.

On occasions like a birthday or completion of so many years, the employee is recognised and given commemorative gifts; sent on paid holidays with his family, the event celebrated with colleagues participating.

Judiciously, the CEO himself would meet with deserving employees and/or send personalised messages.

Outstanding people are encouraged to participate in activities like lecturing, writing articles, sports and the like and these are publicised.

While the organisation's team member is made to feel important, the organisation itself gets publicity too.

When the employee is treated with importance, he in turn treats others in the field, the public etc., with importance. He too gets bouquets and brickbats and, the latter he attends to pronto. He ensures that, should there be stocks to be replaced for some reason or the other, this is done expeditiously. He realises that the trade has invested in his stocks and therefore, should not suffer more than the minimum time needed. These behavioural aspects are inculcated by concern for the others, which is also good Public Relations.

Distribution System

The distribution system needs to be favourable to the company's product/products. The dealer has to have good words, even praise, for the products. This is essential since many customers seek his advice. One can see this happening in pharmacies where the customer seeks the pharmacist's advice and recommendation.

With the distribution chain, long-term relationships are to be built. This implies one needs to know the trade and its problems very closely and be in constant communications with the chain.

An organisation undertakes many measures such as:

(i) Dealer bulletins.

(ii) Greeting cards on birthdays/anniversaries etc., of people.

(iii) Personalised letters.

(iv) Conferences/Workshops.

(v) Recognition through Awards/Certificates etc.

(vi) Training programmes.

(vii) Shares in the company.

(viii) Visits by high officials of the organisation in a programmed way.

(ix) Promotion of art and entertainment.

(x) Publication of books.

(xi) Celebrity endorsement.

(xii) Contests and competitions.

(xiii) Help lines.

(xiv) Media tours.

(xv) Road shows.

In addition, either the dealer's name is included in the company's advertising or were the dealer to undertake advertising (common in hire purchase/off season advertising), the company would subsidise such efforts. Dealers are also encouraged to participate in local expositions—be it a large exhibition or a **mela** or a fair where the principal subsidises costs.

The advantages of good relations with dealers are (a) good displays of the company's products, (b) dealer recommendation to his customers to buy these brands, assured space for pop material, even dealer boards etc.

The main objective of course will remain the same: building long-term relationships.

The Consumer

The cliché in public relations is, "Nine-tenths doing and one-tenth talking about it." This is applicable to product performance and there is no substitute whatsoever for products that live up to promises.

Organisations endeavour to meet current and future customers. Newspapers organise special contests, financial institutions organise meetings with prospective investors, hospitals organise lectures/free tests and so on and on. All these have the common theme—make the organisation known in a good light.

There are organisations that take part in expositions: large and small exhibitions, melas, fairs etc., with the aim of assessing customer attitudes and their own image vis-a-vis its publics.

Organisations allow final year students visit their facilities. An ice cream factory in Vermont, Ben & Jerry, has made its facility as a tourist attraction. Visitors are charged a fee and taken around the factory (with an audio visual screened) and treated to their ice cream. There is a Question and Answer session. Children are given gifts like pencils and balloons and they could buy T shirts/Caps etc., at a highly subsidised cost. In addition, the factory outlet offers visitors gifts/concessional prices were they to buy the products.

The Product

A brand of aerated soft drink has automatic vending machines in sports grounds of schools and colleges and the brand name is prominent. A school specifies a particular pattern of clothing as uniform, made by only one Mill. In an entertainment park, an engine goes around carrying carloads of children and the name of the engine is a chewing gum. On occasions like say the New Year Eve, Clubs offer special gifts donated by organisations, including air tickets and holidays.

Scholarships galore are given in the name of products/companies. Brand ambassadors are appointed for a consideration. Celebrities endorse products (a Public Relations effort) and this is extensively promoted (marketing communications effort).

All these and more are public relations exercises to boost the image of the product/organisation.

Damage Control: Public Relations exercises are undertaken to contain damage to the name of a product. Here is a case: In a Far Eastern country, there was a sudden rumour that a particular brand of toothpaste had an ingredient that offended the majority community. Sales slumped. Here, immediate research established that someone of repute had made this remark and it spread like wild fire. However, it was far from true. To get over the damage, the organisation had to mount a PR exercise. It took the top authorities of the concerned government regulatory agency as also media experts and showed them the manufacturing process—and where and how the ingredients get added and the final product made. There was very wide coverage and authorities certified that people should ignore the rumour and the product had only permitted ingredients (they also gave the names of the ingredients). The organisation made reprints and circulated these widely through the friendly distribution chain and through educational institutions. Educational institutions were also invited to bring students to see for themselves.

It took quite an effort and expense but the damage was overcome and the product in fact enjoyed an increased share of the market. In India, such rumours do crop up from time to time, for example on detergent cakes used and even on salt! They die soon enough because organisations are vigilant. Another problem in India comprises duplicate goods made and sold by unscrupulous people. Here, educating and keeping the trade in good humour, actions are taken to contain this threat. Yet, one can find products with almost similar pack and similar sounding names in rural markets.

Industry Product Problem: Good Public Relations consultants can also come out with answers to products made by many manufacturers in the same industry. Here is a case that is both unusual and innovative:

Whisky made in the US had acquired the name Bourbon. This is malt-based and reddish in colour. The brand leader at that time in the US happened to Grant followed by Daniel and Schenley. After World War II, Bourbon sales were pushed back by Scotch Whisky, golden in colour, smoother in taste and heavily promoted by the makers in Scotland.

The industry had to overcome the problem and the Chairman of Schenley thought that the situation was one of "Do or Die". On behalf of the industry, he called for innovative ideas from good consultants. This demanded a bit of Research. Sequentially, what happened because of this effort ran like this:

(i) The Bourbon Institute of America was founded.

(ii) For the inauguration of this institute, the mass media was flown in by helicopters (a novelty of that period) and, along with celebrities, tasted the American product.

(iii) The industry ensured that Bottle Shops, Hotels, Bars and Duty free shops in Airports were kept informed, their cooperation got—and they stocked/prominently displayed the Bourbon made in different brands by different makers. For the effort with the industry, a well-planned campaign using direct mailers followed by calls etc., were all orchestrated. POPs were made available.

(iv) Sampling was undertaken to the trend setters, icons of that period. Their sipping American Bourbon was publicised by the media extensively.

(v) The Mayor of Dublin hosted a party where Bourbon was served to all dignitaries, who praised the taste.

(vi) The US President, on his trip to the USSR toasted on Bourbon and the President of USSR praised this good drink.

(vii) In Hollywood movies, heroes imbibed Bourbon. In the film **Anatomy of Murder,** instead of Rye mentioned in the book version, the hero promotes Bourbon.

(viii) Stars like Red Skeleton praised Bourbon.

These exercises put the industry in the black, helped them obtain a fair share of the US market and in addition, get into overseas markets.

Good innovative opportunities can be missed too! Here is an example. At a time when we had foreign exchange crunch and it was not known that tobacco caused cancer, the Tobacco Export Promotion Council invited innovative suggestions to "export" Indian **beedis** to the US. The plus points were since the **beedi** was wrapped in tendu leaf and contained very little tobacco, it could be sold at a fraction of the cost of cigarettes. It was also a "natural" product, hand rolled.

The American associate of the Agency for TEC looked at the problem. The Beatles were yet to make it big and they suggested persuading the Beatles to smoke Indian **beedis** and set the trend. The cost was negligible. However, red tape killed this idea and the project did not take off.

Abuse of PR: The tobacco giants (until a whistle blower revealed everything), for a long time, were using PR power to mislead/ suppress the harmful effects of tobacco and accepted responsibility only when confronted with facts provided by the whistle blower. This could be termed misuse of PR.

Whatever the problem be, the consideration for using PR in marketing communications are its advantages, namely:

(i) It is less expensive and often gets free media exposure.

(ii) Media comments are taken as more authoritative than claims in advertising.

(iii) PR can cut through advertising noise/clutter, supplement efforts in a different manner and impact more.

(iv) PR is more credible.

(v) PR can generate sales leads—the trade is always looking at new products and opportunities and write for more information upon seeing news.

(vi) In some cases—because of the legal constraints among others —PR can be the only means of reaching the public.

Publicity

The dictionary gives the meaning of publicity as "being open to general observation/notoriety or the business of advertising (goods or persons)". To the professional, however, publicity is mere information that may either impact or otherwise.

For example, a minister's tour programme is publicity. On the other hand, an icon opening a new retail showroom, although publicity, may bring in some customers. A famous author selling autographed books at launch is also publicity.

The point about publicity (in the professional sense) is that it can be free news item or a paid for advertisement.

The goals of publicity in marketing communications would be:

(i) **Merchandising:** This will include events geared towards direct sales. Inviting a celebrity with whom customers can chat or have lunch or whatever is an example

(ii) **Entertainment:** The purpose of publicity is to earn goodwill. As an example, one can cite companies organising Diwali celebrations where crackers are burst—and this is more in the nature of community relations.

(iii) **Community involvement:** Blood donation drives, donating an ambulance van, offering kiosks to rehabilate wounded jawans and the like would be good examples.

Despite the foregoing, in marketing the word publicity is almost always confused with advertising or public relations.

Summary

Publicity is a free news about a corporate or a brand. The news can give a positive or a negative edge to the image of the brand. While it has no cost attached to it, the corporate has no control over it.

Public relations is a planned effort by a corporate to create a favourable opinion about the brand to its stake holders. It involves a budget. Several tools are available for creating a favourable image through public relations. Some of the frequently used tools are Press conference, sponsorship of events, supporting socially beneficial projects, and recognition of loyal customers etc.

Keywords

- Publicty
- Public Relations

Discussion Question

1. Distinguish between publicity and public relations.

15

Personal Selling

15

Personal Selling

Role of Company Sales Force

Selling is a great art. **The Guinness Book of World Records** has, for 12 consecutive years, chosen a used car salesman as the best salesman. Interviewed, he stated that he never makes a sale. He makes friends and understands their problem. Then he provides the right solution but does not stop at that. He keeps in touch with them and ensures that when some of them upgrade to a newer car, his services are used. Because of the word of mouth referral he gets, no wonder he was chosen the best in the world!

The sales force forms an asset to the organisation. Good organisations choose the right persons and in so doing, "communicate" with that person—not "with reference to your application" but "we are delighted that you have written to us and you may be the person we are on the look out to join our family." Right from the first opportunity, the art of communication is used and inculcated. The right environment makes the sales person assimilate the corporate and marketing philosophies of the organisation and he would be treated as the ambassador for the product and the company. Out there in the market, his face is the face of the organisation. (We had mentioned this under Public Relations earlier).

Sales function would differ according to the type of organisation, since some are in consumer perishables, some consumer durables, some in services, some in industry, business, commerce, and so on.

The first thing an organisation ensures is thorough training of the sales team, followed by refresher courses at intervals and providing the team with updates through email, letters, literature, CDs etc.

Sales personnel must have thorough knowledge of:

(i) The product—what it does, how it is made, why it is made and so on.

(ii) The Market—physical, the actual users, their geographics, demographics, psychographics etc.

(iii) Changes that take place all the time.

(iv) The legal aspects/ethics.

(v) The distribution chain.

(vi) How goods reach the chain: from depots to agents to retailers and to consumers.

(vii) The competition—strengths and weaknesses.

(viii) The promotion plans, schedules etc.

The sales team is also a potent communication medium. For consumer perishables (an airline seat is a perishable since if it is not sold before departure of the flight, it goes waste) or durables there is a level of pressure in selling. There is also intense competition. The mettle of the sales person is revealed in such challenging situations —and that is where he becomes a successful communication medium.

In the case of industrial products, now called B2B or Business to Business products, the requirement may include a technical degree so that the representative could talk and understand technical requirements. In the case of medical products too there may be need for a science or pharma degree in order to be able to talk better to the medical professionals.

In both fields, there may be need to give advice (pre-sale) and there will certainly be need for follow up (after sales service).

Where products or services are offered directly to the target audience, and if the effort uses broadcast, TV Marketing the sales force performs what is known as 'Direct Marketing' or 'Response Marketing'.

All costs of marketing, including advertising, public relations, publicity, sales promotion etc., are met out of the marketing budget.

One of the components of the marketing budget is the costs of sales personnel.

In the case of B2B, as high as 70% or more of the budget goes for direct marketing.

In the case of consumer products, this is somewhere around 30%

The duties of the field force would include:

(i) Salesmanship.
(ii) Public relations.
(iii) Publicity.
(iv) Customer relations.
(v) Market research/market intelligence gathering.
(vi) Demonstration.
(vii) Follow up.

The functions of the field force would include:

(i) Finding prospects.
(ii) Converting prospects into customers.
(iii) Maintaining and building relationships.
(iv) Establishing market leadership.
(v) Utilising all the support given to sales efforts.

Those engaged in consumer expendables contact stockists, agents, wholesalers, retail outlets etc., and wherever opportunity affords, actual consumers. Sometimes they also meet bulk consumers.

The primary job of the sales force is promotion in every sense of the word. Different from advertising, the character of their job will be:

(i) Their communication will be dyadic. This means "paired" or face to face or one-to-one (interpersonal) communications. There will always be opportunities to (a) introduce new features, (b) new products, (c) new schemes and the like when the sales force could meet groups of his audience and make presentations. Even otherwise, as a PR exercise, sales force meets groups of retailers/stockists etc., over a cup of tea from time to time.

(ii) There is direct and immediate interaction.

(iii) The message strategies can be adopted/adapted to suit diverse levels and different situations.

(iv) Questions can be answered on the spot.

Today, the emphasis on HR is such that every good organisation ensures training and retraining. At the time of recruitment, the sales force is thoroughly trained and thereafter exposed to refresher courses. Periodically or continually, they are also assessed for strengths and weaknesses—if there are weaknesses, they are counselled/given training. Deserving personnel are also sent for advanced courses so that they can rise in the organisation heirarchy. The sales force is also encouraged to participate in outside activities/competitions etc.

The training received by the sales force enables them to:

(a) Make thorough preparation—well in advance—of making contact with a prospect.

(b) Make appointments.

(c) Make the presentation.

(d) Overcome barriers.

(e) Stimulate interest.

(f) Create the need.

(g) Make a sale.

(h) Follow up, personally, over the phone, e-mail or regular mail.

(i) Build relationship.

(j) Intelligently blend efforts with other marketing communication efforts/promotion programmes.

(k) Give meaningful feedback to the organisation.

(l) Be proactive.

Necessarily, the sales force is provided with presentation aids, in the form of:

(a) Flip charts.

(b) Literature.

(c) Technical/Service data.

(d) Price list/terms and conditions.

(e) Audio visual cassettes/slides/power point presentations.

(f) Other help.

It needs to be noted that industrial/pharmaceutical products too require the same planning methodology. It is only in the media selection/support material etc. that the stress and relevance would vary.

Summary

Personal selling is one of the most important components of commercial mix. Personal selling involves promotion of a product/ service by a sales person to a prospect/customer. Application of personal selling exists in all kinds of products in varying degrees. However, we can say that personal selling is more commonly used in industrial marketing/IT/Health care.

Keywords

- Personal Selling
- B2B selling

Discussion Question

1. Contrast the role of personal selling with that of advertising.

16

Advertising over Internet

16

Advertising over Internet

Introduction

When the first computer was built (around late 1950s/ early 1960s), it was immense in size/cost and used punchcards and the world wide demand was reckoned as just the number of fingers on one hand!

However, new IT technology, ideas, tools gadgets etc., particularly since late 1980s saw the advent of the personal computer, fiber optics, micro processor, cd rom and much more.

Three major happenings—both since 1989 in IT—have contributed to the creation of a new way of marketing and advertising. The first is the PC or personal computer, the second the W3 or www or worldwide web and the third being Internet providers. This was followed by optic fibre and then nano-technology by way of smaller chips/ handy instruments etc.

In March 1989, Sir Tim Berners Lee proposed an outline and, soon joined by; others saw the birth of the World Wide Web. This in turn gave way to creation of web sites and available free via the Internet (Providers are plenty) and accessible to everyone with a PC, the usage today is in every language without border worldwide.

Many of these recent developments are victims of technological obsolescence and today (this could have changed even when you are reading this!) the IT world comprise Laptops, Note Books, 3G (the 4G is on its way) cellphones. Today communication is very fast and instant.

The low cost of a PC/cellphone has seen an explosive and increasing number of PC (laptop/notebook) owners. BBC estimated ownership by 2010 at 1.3 billion worldwide. India targeted 50 million by end 2010. The main users of these conveniences are the "young" including the student community and the target audience which is mostly young of 20+ age group. This generation takes full advantage of the versatility of the computer from Internet banking, payment of taxes, checking up dates, reading news, watching a movie or a game, chatting with group and friends, getting information and more.

Advantage of the New Technology

Today almost every organisation—in every field—and many individual too—has its own website.

The dynamic development of new IT technologies gained momentum and witnessed, say in the highly competitive but cost escalating airlines business, the offer of cheaper tickets/e-tickets.

The number of users is growing very fast and data/profiles of these users are available from several sources including the network provider. Specialists for creations of interactive websites for every type of marketer/product/service came on the scene and the medium offered many benefits sought by advertiser and the customers alike. These include:

Readily available data of the target group—all over the world and/or in specific geographical areas.

Interaction—a dialogue can take place.

Information—"live demo" of product/technical data/availability/ pricing/terms etc.

Cross references— (in many cases) of other source/blogs / frequently asked questions/satisfied customers etc.

So, much so when one opens his/her e-mail, up pops advertisement —for products/services/investment opportunities/job and what have you.

The "in" box of the e-mail includes several mails which are actually advertisements/offers/requests.

The advertising rates are currently attractive and offered for a period of time or on the basis of "hits" meaning every time the source is contacted.

In the US, airlines in highly competitive price war situation offered attractive fares on direct booking (paid instantly by credit card) in order to do away with agents. (agent is never the less retained and are fee to charge a fee on the customer). In India too, we have the facility of booking air/rail/bus/cab services online. Hotel booking/ property and buying and selling of every thing (see e-Bay), auctions —nothing is away from the computer keyboard!

India: In February 2010, Arun Thadanki. MD of Yahoo told to **The Hindu** at the CII Brand summit.

Ad spend on the net is fast changing

Last year Internet's share was Rs.600 crore.

The number of regular Internet users in the 25 plus age group is 2.2 crore.

Advertisers could opt for and reach specific group such as cricket fans/personal care product user/fitness conscious and so on.

The estimated number of net browsers in our country is astonishing at 50 million people presently.

The net's advantage have already been recognised and used by banks, offering online links to various services, car makers.

The growth rate over network advertising is now 35% a year.

There are some 12 million cellphones in use in India is the use of Internet advertising would also have a bearing on government polices like the new generation 3G cellphones.

Internet advertising complies with government/local regulations.

Internet advertising has also attracted criticism, (**Sevanthi Ninan in The Hindu**) for the net (till recently) enable personal expression. Social media is criticised for it's "Sharing" list of contacts, other details, and personal blogs—all for promoting the self. Ms Ninan observes, "One marvels at the way marketing tends to inveigle itself in to all kind of communication spaces...from interactivity to self-promotion, to insidious selling."

Interactive Advertising

Internet and interactive media services. Dell sells more computers through Internet than regular retail outlets. Amazon is a successful retailer of books on Internet. Opportunities for marketing communication have opened up on Internet.

Internet Advertising

In terms of efficiency, the advertising industry is now starting to rise out of its century-long infancy. The new era of innovative advertising can be called "the new Wanamaker era". John Wanamaker was a devoutly Christian merchant from Philadelphia, who in the 1870s not only invented department stores and price tags but also became the first modern advertiser. He was the first advertiser who bought space in newspapers to promote his chain of stores. He brought a much needed revolution in the advertising world. A few years ago, when the Internet hit the market, advertising industry got a new medium. And soon whole advertising world was taken by storm in capitalising on this media.

According to a recent advertising industry survey, it was revealed that Internet advertising will be generating $ 428 billion revenues this year. This is a whooping amount in comparison to the previous year's $ 220 billion. It has been now proved that approximately 21 per cent of Internet users consider online advertising relevant. Internet advertising has overtaken other traditional advertising media such as newspapers, magazines and radio.

With new platforms for advertising evolving on a continual basis, choosing the right medium is more and more difficult. By having a solid understanding of certain aspects of Internet advertising, companies can find the right media mix that works. To achieve success in Internet advertising, a clear knowledge of the basics of Internet functioning is essential. Additionally, understand that some media can work better than others depending on type of customers and the products offered. Internet advertising would work wonders if the customer base can be from any part of the world and transaction can be handled well over the Internet. It also works well with certain types of products and services and also depends on certain regions. While Internet advertising can directly relate to sales, it can have huge effectiveness on exercises of brand awareness, recognition and networking.

Majority of business owners worldwide know that the Internet has now become an essential tool when it comes to running their businesses successfully. However, you should also understand the role played by the Internet in the lives of their customers. You should be capable to locate people who are using the Internet; their key interests in the time spend on the Internet and their preferences to purchase products and services on a daily basis.

Business

The information highway cannot be ignored by marketers. Internet has become a powerful tool not only for information sourcing but also for personal communication through e-mail. For business, it has opened new methods for marketing products and services. Traditional media like print and broadcasting provide one way access to the prospects. Marketers use these media to create brand awareness, brand image building, relationship with customer etc. However, there is considerable time lag for feedback/response from the customers. Internet provides opportunity for live interaction with the customers through links. The traditional media like print and broadcasting are addressable media whereas Internet is an interactive media.

Interactive media has following distinguishing features which separates it from mass media:

(i) Targetting of customers is very focused.

(ii) The company can talk to customers in real time.

(iii) Customisation of messages is possible.

(iv) The results are easily measurable.

(v) Costs are relatively low.

(vi) It can be used for all kinds of products and services.

Following are the online advertising options:

(a) **Banners:** This is the most common form of advertising on the web. It can be used for creating awareness or recognition or direct marketing objectives. Though the present response is low in the future banner advertisement may become important mode of advertisement.

(b) **Pop-ups/Pop-unders:** Pop-ups appear when we access a particular site on Internet. Pop-unders appear underneath the webpage. This is visible when one is exiting the web page.

(c) **Interstitials:** These are ads which appear when we are waiting for a site to open. Research indicates that these ads have higher recalls than pop-up.

(d) **Push technologies:** Also called 'web casting technologies'. Companies push their message to customers. These ads come as a hook to sites which the viewer is exploring for information.

(e) **Sponsorship:** Many a times, sites are supported by sponsorship. If sponsor pays for maintaining contents of site and in return gets exposure for his brand.

Presently in our country most Internet advertising is used as a supplement to traditional mass advertising. However, the future lies in this medium.

Benefits of Advertising

(i) Internet advertising is huge: With the growth of information on the Internet has growth the amount of time people spend on it, which has in turn generated a new market for Internet advertising. Some of the wealthiest companies in the world have made sure that they get a piece of the internet marketing pie, and for a good reason.

(ii) Internet advertising is targeted: As a company looking for advertising opportunities to a specific market, Internet advertising offers some targeting methods that insure that those who see your ads are the ones most likely to buy. Programmes like Google's AdWords and AdSense match up advertisers with content that their target market peruses regularly. Forget the costly machine-gun strategy of newspaper advertisements, Internet advertising is targeted!

(iii) Internet adverting enables good conversion tracking: It is impossible to get a good idea of how many people see advertising through traditional means. Tracking the reach of newspaper and television advertisments is difficult. However, Internet advertising allows the advertiser to track the number of impressions an ad gets (how many people see it), and how many visits their business web site gets from particular ads, making it easy to see what kind of conversion rates internet advertisements are getting.

(iv) Internet advertising has a lower entry-level fees: If you have a limited budget, Internet advertising can be much more in reach than traditional methods. A small yellow-page ad can cost thousand rupees. However, you can bid for advertisements on Google and Overture on a performance basis. That means that you only get charged when visitors click on the advertisement, and bidding starts at a few rupees pop.

(v) Internet advertising can be much cheaper

Because of the targeted nature of Internet advertising and the ability to track the effectiveness of ads, conversion rates from internet advertising is typically much better than traditional mediums.

(vi) Internet advertising has greater range

One more benefit is that, since the Internet spans the globe, pockets of your target market scattered around the world can all be targetted at once, rather than trying to find different publications, radio stations and television stations that cater to a particular geographical area.

On the whole, Internet advertising can be a great way to get the word out there about your service or product in a cost-effective, efficient way.

Limitations

(i) **Measurement problem:** It is difficult to measure effectiveness of advertising.

(ii) **Surfing speed:** Due to traffic and technical difficulties users find that the time required to access sites can be long.

(iii) **Clutters:** Too many ads over a short period could result in low registration of the message.

(iv) **Privacy:** Like telephones being misused for telemarketing, Internet is also accused of invading user privacy.

Summary

Internet has become a powerful alternative to traditional media. Though still in a nascent stage, Internet advertising has a promising future. While Internet as a stand alone channel for advertising is questionable, it has a role by integrating with other components of marketing communication.

Keywords

- Internet
- Micro processor
- Interactive media
- Pop-under
- Information highway
- CD Rom
- Banner advertisements
- Link
- Fibre optics
- World wide web
- Pop-ups
- Interstitials

Discussion Question

1. Discuss trends in Internet advertising.

17

Point of Purchase or Point of Sale

17

Point of Purchase or Point of Sale

The two terms denote the same thing but from two different viewpoints. The place where customers make their purchases is the point of purchase and for the company offering the product the place where a sale is made by a shopkeeper is the point of sale.

Place Where Sales are Made

The shopping mall, the theme park, etc., are great spectacles. The main aim of these places is to pull crowds and the crowds go there for getting "value for money". The Mall in America got started because, with rise in incomes and mobility—everyone had a car to move around—people started building residences miles away from shopping centres in cities. The people who conceptualised the malls (as they do even to this day) studied existing architecture, people's psychology etc. before building their malls.

Fig. 17.1: An example of in-shop poster

The places they studied were religious. People are awed at the towering **gopurams** in India as they do of church/steeples in other countries. They can see these from a great distance and when they stand nearby, the towers seem to have no end and appear to touch the skies. The architecture extends to the walls, the sculptures, the ceilings inside, the pillars, all leading to the finale—the icon of worship. Then the study includes the flow of people from one attraction to another inside the place of worship. Lighting and the sounds of bells, the way prayers are told etc., are also studied.

The mall is built on a theme and the only aim is to make the driver of any vehicle pull up, park in the parking lot and enter the mall. So the mall has a theme and attractions other than shopping. It also has food courts and conveniences. It is open on weekends and holidays and so makes an ideal place to visit on holidays—more as an outing or even a picnic.

The Victoria Terminus (built on the site of a temple) in Mumbai was built after studying the architcture of India and it had to be a spectacular building. In the event, it is gigantic and a blend of European and Indian architecture.

The shopping areas are designed after taking consumer psychology into reckoning. The display, décor, colour scheme, lighting, music in the background, the livery, etc., and the display aids—in the windows, walls etc., increase impact. These are backed by well-trained, well-dressed employees (who ask, May I help you?) and the layout is such that the customer goes through different attractions. The pricey ones have more display room and are specially displayed while the inexpensive items are crowded and take the lower shelves in display areas. Mannequins and even live models are used. For clothing, enough trial rooms are provided. In the US, there is always a kind of sale on and people who go for an outing—to spend time away from home, looking at fountains or other attractions in a mall end up shopping!

Then there are chain stores, company/factory outlets and franchise outlets. All have the same colour scheme, theme, arrangement, décor, livery etc. These are all arranged to instill confidence in the audience, which travels around. Even though a local store or fast food place could be far better, because of heavy promotion and familiarity, the consumer would prefer the "trusted" place because he is familiar with that brand.

It should be noted that exclusive outlets such as company shops/ franchised ones also help in feedback and in modern times a data base for considering relationship marketing.

Then there are seasonal displays and attractions. Here again, there is uniformity of material used.

One good example in our country would be the Bata showrooms. Here, one can see—from the signboard outside to the display and décor—uniformity. The window and other displays change to suit the needs of the time. When schools reopen, the theme attracts this occasion/when Christmas and New Year season nears, the display changes. So it is with Diwali and, regionally, with Pongal, Pooja etc.

There is need to study the Point of Sale (outlet) as a theme by itself.

Point of Sale Material

Customers enter shops with a preconceived idea of buying specific objects. How does one make them buy a specific brand?

The entire gamut of marketing communications aims at the sale by bringing the customer into the shop and demand a brand by name. Therefore, whatever the manufacturer can do to clinch a sale, he needs to ensure that at the point of sale. Point of sale takes different shapes:

Dealer board: Where the product is illustrated along with the slogan and the dealer's name added. This could be illuminated, neonised signs, glow signs, etc.

In-shop sign: There could be lighted or plain boards within a shop too. (common inside bars since liquor advertising is not encouraged very much outdoors in many states).

Product displays: Floor/Shelf/Window can be utilised for special displays, including for gift seasons such as Diwali/Christmas and days like Mothers day ,Fathers day , Valentine etc. The display could be mechanised and made very attractive.

While displaying the angle of the eye from which the product can be seen is taken into account and display, being primarily eye-appeal, ensures maximum viewership. The height of the display props and the placement of the product itself need careful study.

Dispensers: A special display (large size) pack is used to dispense unit packs—which is found to be useful for small sized products (say chewing gums or round shaped shoe polishes). Another type of display dispenser is the tear-off bubble packs of toothbrushes, betel nut, shampoo etc., (as sachets).

Display aids: Blow up of photographs, blown-up dummy package, posters, showcards, stickers, crowners, tin plates, etc., are used as display aids to promote the product.

Other in-store advertising such as moving signs, closed circuit television screening commercials, announcements over PA systems, and more are normal in larger outlets.

Purpose of POPs: The purpose of point of purchase or sale is the same as that of the package. Cash in on the consumer buying philosophy by attracting and enhancing the appeal. The pack/brand and the aura created by POPs is the one that attracts the customer's eye and through the eye his purse.

How do POPs work?

These work in three ways:

(i) As a reminder: Almost everyone visiting a shop looks at displays and the point of sale material. Through other marketing communications, the customer may already be aware of the product but may not remember—in the shop the display/pop reminds him.

(ii) Stimulates impulse purchase: A large section of customers go shopping with something in mind but end up buying things they had not thought of—because of the display, schemes etc.

Studies in chain stores and malls reveal that impulse buying is steadily growing—because, in a self service situation, the customer spends more time looking at product lines, going around and is in a fairly relaxed mood too. This same customer, when visiting shops where the shopkeeper/assistants take orders, needs to wait doing nothing and is quite happy to read out a list of things he wants. He does not spend time looking at other attractions. In such situations, impulse buying dips.

(iii) Shelf space: The purpose of marketing communications is to help the movement of the product from the shelves of the retail outlets. Towards this aim, the advertiser spends on multimedia and the ultimate test is in the retail outlet. Therefore, effective displays at this point, where the action takes place, are essential. Organisations ensure that promotional incentives offered to retail outlets take the element of good displays into reckoning. By doing so, the manufacturer also aims at containing competition to the maximum possible extent.

POPs could be year round and also related to specific festive or other seasons. There is need to plan pops very carefully and organise the mix in such a way that they play an effective and decisive part in marketing communications.

Summary

Promotion at the place where sales takes place is gaining in importance. Point of Purchase and Point of Sales are different nomenclatures used but mean the same thing. Several tools are used at Point of Purchase to promote sales. Some of these are Dealer Board, In-shop sign, Product Displays, Dispensers, Display Aids etc. Point of Purchase Promotions work as reminders and also stimulate impulse purchases.

Keywords

- Point of purchase
- Point of sales
- In-shop signs
- Dealer board
- Product displays
- Dispensers
- Display aids

Discussion Question

1. Discuss the significance of role of Point of Purchase Promotion.

18

Marketing Communication for Industrial Products

18

Marketing Communication for Industrial Products

The term Industrial Marketing, until the last century, included all products used by an industry. This now includes (a) capital equipment in the form of plants and machinery, (b) raw material, (c) aids like computers, communication items including telephones etc. and (d) services such as equipment maintenance, servicing, repairs etc. Some of these are also called B2B.

Industrial goods produce consumer goods or are used in areas that benefit the consumer—for example, radar that is used for weather forecasts, spotting and guiding aircraft and also for defence purposes.

Many items used in industry are also used in homes: energy, communication equipment, washing and cleaning items, building material, security items, transport, etc.

Many former professions and businesses are today called 'industries'. Thus, tourism is an industry. While civil aviation and shipping, which transport goods and people are industries, the railways and surface transportation (trucks and buses) are called 'services'.

In India, we also have the classifications: rural industries/ urban industries or cottage, small–scale industries, medium industries, large industries. In addition, we have public sector, private sector and public private partnership. There are also government departments at the centre and states, which are responsible for infrastructure and other areas.

In a global marketplace, today we are producing industrial (and all other) goods in as economical manner as possible. Thus if we take steel, ore is shipped to another country where it is made into steel; clothing in many global brands are made in several countries; famous footwear, because of cheap labour, are made in China.

The characteristics of industrial goods include (i) the demand is derived, (ii) Some demands are joint: for example, use of a raw material and needed energy in the form of say oil or coke, and (iii) subject to vagaries of nature—for example if there is a shortage of cotton, the textile industry is affected.

In the same industry, although we generally call it by one name, there are several industries. For example, if we talk of textile industry, it includes silk, woolen, rayon and cotton fabrics. It also takes us through ginning mills, yarn mills, weaving mills, bleaching facilities, carding facilities and so on as also power looms, hand looms etc. If we take only woven clothing, we have silk, wool, cotton, synthetics, mixtures, linen and so on.

There is also technical obsolescence that is taking place at a fast pace in some industries such as IT, aviation and defence.

The industrial market cannot be distinguished by goods alone but industrial users have three points of difference:

(i) Goods are purchased as a means to an economic end – to reduce costs while improving quality and profits.

(ii) Goods are produced for non-economic reasons such as for social or political purposes.

(iii) In industrial markets, goods are not bought for themselves but only for the contributions they can make to the economic, social or political objectives of the purchasers. As an example, a buyer of a two-wheeler may buy a good seat for its own worth. On the other hand, the two-wheeler manufacturer is concerned only with the contribution made by the seat to his production facility and the saleability—through value addition. The well-being of the purchaser is what helps the two wheeler manufacturer.

People addressed in industrial marketing communications are:

(i) Purchasing agents/buyers

(ii) Engineers, technicians, technocrats, workers

(iii) Top management

(iv) Regulatory authorities who may insist on using what they have approved

(v) In the case of governments, the pressure groups, the diplomatic channels etc.

In order to "sell", the organisation may directly contact, may have agents/representatives, and where the product line is used widely, have distribution chains.

Irrespective of who does the marketing, marketing is by people who call on people. Their communications are product-related, industry-related, market-related, price-related and service (pre- and post-) related. The presentations are one on one or to groups by one person or a team of experts.

Take today's aviation sector. The big players, Boeing and Airbus, both vie with each other in selling, in their language, a better than the other product. In so doing, they include studies of the industry, the market, the service, the pricing. They also undertake sales promotion by buying existing ageing fleet of aircraft, training, financing and other attractive terms.

Industry Related: Depending upon the industry, the product/ services-range offer their products. For example, in creating a modern airport, the number of systems, related equipment, service, training etc., is enormous.

Market Relations: The size and geographical concentration of the market may consist of just one or two buyers, say for an atomic reactor or a steel plant or for ship building etc. These require plants that are specially tailor-made.

The buyers for some other products could run into thousands. For example, trolleys or computers or industrial sewing machines.

Derived Demand: The demand for industrial products is, ultimately, decided by demand at the consumer levels. Without any demand for products and services/conveniences at the level of consumers, there will be no demand for industrial products. Therefore the industrial manufacturer takes cognizance of consumer trends/demands in the planning. One may quote the example of studies in air travel. These indicate that there is a dramatic increase in travel, which will continue, in countries such as India, China and other Eastern ones.

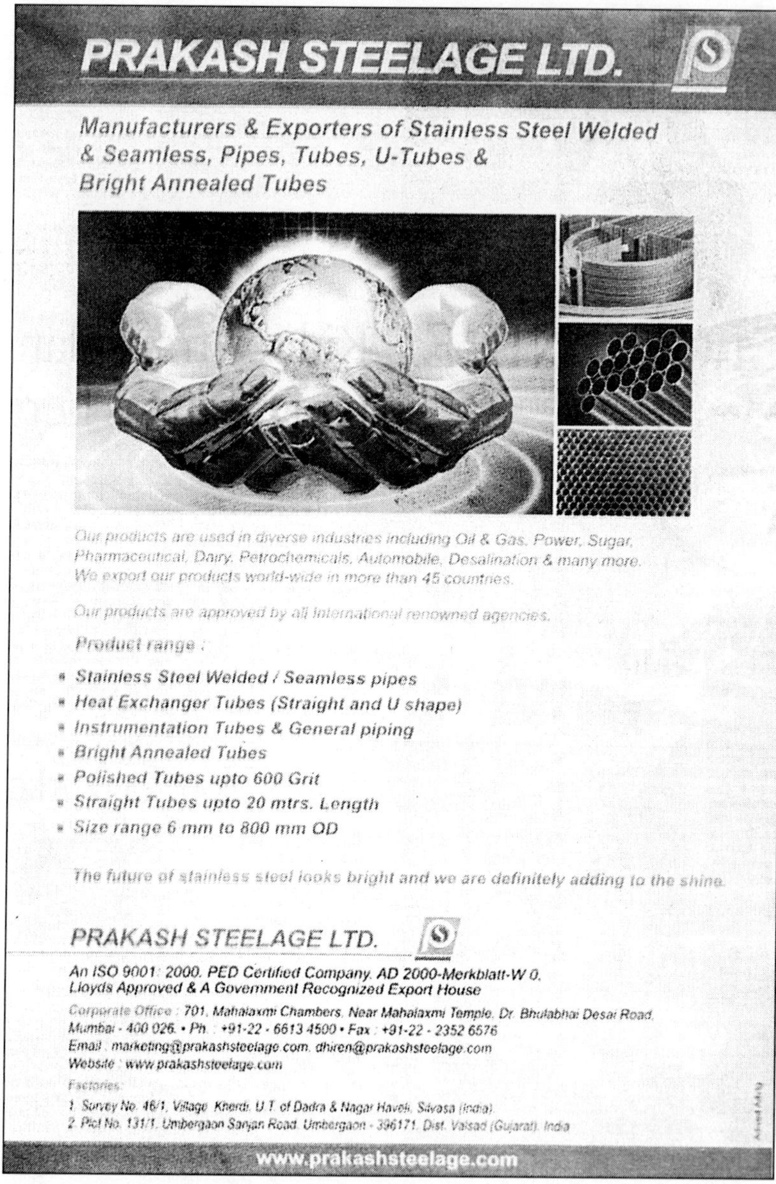

Fig.18.1: Prakash Steels advertises for a range of industrial raw materials

Economic/Political Features: Aside from the foregoing, the following too need to be borne in mind:

- Political stability of the country

- Investment attitudes
- Technical maturity levels

Replacement and new equipment etc., have a market because of economic urgency or where the competition takes the lead.

Capability, a strength, is not necessarily a weighty plus. It has no meaning when the equipment is a standard one and there is hardly any differentiation between the products except perhaps the price/terms.

Demarcation: The potential buyers are clearly known in industrial marketing. Equally well known are the motivation and parameters for purchase. It is also known that not technological obsolescence but economical obsolescence is the key in upgrading/modernising equipment.

Where new users/uses can be found, the market for industrial products can be expanded. However, if the market is fixed, it would be impossible to grow and every single order becomes important.

Goals of Marketing Communications

The basic goals are no different from those for consumer products, i.e., creating awareness, interest, favourable attitude etc., leading to placing the orders.

The differences lie in (a) the audience being technically qualified, it is also trained to evaluate, (b) emotional approaches as in consumer advertising will not work. Solid reason is required. The size of the audience is small . However, industrial advertising is visually getting more appealing.

Inputs: We first need to know the segmentation variables, which are:

Descriptive: These include type of industry, geographic location, size etc.

Operating: Refers to customer's technological sophistication levels, past usage status, capabilities in operating technical areas, purchasing practices—formal organisation, Internal structure of power, nature of organisational relationships, policies, criteria and applied and the like.

Situational: Urgency of purchase, specific application of the product, size of order or part of the order etc.

People: Characteristics of decision makers, including buyer-seller familiarity, motivation, individual percepts and risk management strategies.

Technology: High end, how complex

Price: High or what

Channel: Just the buyer? Agent? Dealer?

Information: In industrial purchases, buyers, in particular the decision makers, seek and get a lot of information and go through prolonged processes for evaluating and making decisions. The same people, who at home are no different from others, in the work place are serious minded experts. Unlike in consumer advertising, they react favourably only where there is transparent honesty and even understatement. At home they are relaxed while at work they are serious minded and devoted to their task.

The Manager of Crucible Steels in the US has summarised some basic principles to be followed in communications, which include:

(i) Information must be factual.

(ii) Marketing communications must feature:

  (a) Applications of the equipment in actual use
  (b) Technical data in support of claims/features
  (c) Cost
  (d) Availability—lead time needed
  (e) Cost
  (f) Economy and ROI
  (g) Offer of more technical information
  (h) Services in the field
  (i) Demonstration (or visit to site where such equipment is in use or showing live over the company web, television monitors, and including tele-conferencing)
  (j) Name or address of person who would contact/who could be contacted for further information and progress.

Personal efforts need to be supported and integrated with other forms of communications. Such integrated communications have impact and results are favourable. In the US, John Morris did a study He interviewed over a hundred thousand technical people over 26 business/industrial product lines at over 30,000 locations and sites. His conclusive findings were that integrated marketing communications were more effective than just personal contacts and visits.

Media to be used would include presentations using latest equipment by an expert team to the client and his team, tele-conferencing if needed, technical literature, profile of the organisation and may be giveaways.

Marketing communications for technical and industrial products are a very small percentage of sales values.

Summary

Personal selling is the major component of promotion mix used in communication for industrial products. Advertising is used as a supplement to personal selling.

The basic goals are no different in industrial marketing as compared to consumer products marketing i.e., creating awareness, interest, favourable attitude etc., leading to the buying of the products.

The differences lie in the audience who is technically qualified. Emotional approaches used in consumer advertising will not work in industrial marketing.

Keywords

- Technical obsolescence
- Derived demand

Discussion Question

1. Distinguish between approaches to Communication for consumer products and communication for Industrial products.

19

Corporate or Institutional Communications

19

Corporate or Institutional Communications

The term institution covers not only mental or religious ones but political, individual, social, educational, corporate and other institutions.

Corporate communications is, in fact, "organising expressions." Such expressions would be built around the image of the corporate body.*

Corporate communications is used to "Position" the organisation vis-à-vis its specific target audiences. Unlike marketing communications, corporate communications establish understanding at a "rational" level. This is also termed 'strategic' communications.

A corporate body attains its own personality the way it is nurtured over a period of time. We normally talk of organisations the same way we talk of people and use adjectives such as solid, dependable, good, bad and so on.

In its nascent stages, an organisation offers a product or service and when it establishes itself over a time frame, the organisation itself becomes a brand. Its products/ services and the name of the company get synergised. It is around this time, the management tends to believe that the name of the company has accrued value. Image building exercises including corporate advertising are undertaken. Thereafter, with some amount of confidence, the company may (a) offer public issues with success,

---

*At this point, please do refer to earlier chapters on Public Relations from the viewpoint of marketing communications.

(b) introduce new lines, which may or may not succeed. In fact, one MNC—dominating the market with its soaps did not succeed with food lines but later on it bought over other organisations and is now in foods too.

Such efforts can be misused too. Giant corporations in the US—one of which entered energy plants in India as an example—have been found to have misled the public and governments. The tobacco industry consistently misled the audience until a whistle blower set things right on the issue of cancer. The argument to justify such communications is advanced that no organisation exists to be closed!

Such examples are just a few but the majority of organisations are functioning well and their efforts are beyond doubt or question.

Unlike marketing communications where the marketing chief controls the efforts, in the case of corporate advertising, the CEO needs to be involved from concept to execution to accountability. His job is (a) to build the organisation to an unassailable position in the minds of the related publics (b) sustain this image through actions, and (c) take care of the bottom line.

A very long time ago, the **Time Magazine** said this of corporate advertising,

"On a rupee for rupee basis, advertising can convey information as effectively, and less expensively, than nearly anything else you may be currently doing.

"If by using corporate advertising, your salesman gets in to see his prospect a little sooner, if his call becomes a little shorter because the prospect knows much more about him, if the salesman thinks he is more successful and therefore makes himself more successful, if prospective employees seek your company out, if disgruntled employees gain a little more understanding of you, if dissidents speak less harshly, if your competitors speak more respectfully, if the mis-informed learn something, if investors get excited, if legislators become receptive to your line, there will be greater profits."

The above comprehensive statement encompasses all the publics of an organisation as also the community at large. What it all amounts to can be said as follows:

(i) Corporate communications is cost effective.

(ii) Corporate communications can aim at a diverse audience or a specific segment.

(iii) Corporate communications can help various disciplines within the organisation, be it marketing, finance, human resource management.

In our country, corporate communications has been undertaken in a sustained manner by the more enlightened. For example, the house of TATAS have been doing this long before we attained Independence and constitute an outstanding example. In recent times, ITC (earlier Imperial and then India Tobacco Company) has repositioned itself in short name and is today in areas away from tobacco, hospitality, consumer products, garments and so on.

By and large, organisations undertake corporate advertising for strategic reasons: such as before a public issue or to reposition itself, annual or more frequent reporting, some times before a Union or a State Budget to advocate for concessions or relief and so on.

The planning process for corporate advertising will be more or less the same as for consumer advertising. However, as an expert observed, "The choice of media should be determined not by circulation but by influence."

Fig. 19.1: Example of Corporate Communication

Summary

Corporate communication is used to create a favourable view about a company among its various stake holders including customers, employees, government, shareholders and citizens. Corporate communication is a step in building public relations.

Corporate communication is used to reposition itself to market company shares, to negotiate for concessions with government.

Keywords

- Corporate communication
- Nascent stages
- Reposition
- Institutional communication
- Unassailable position

Discussion Question

1. Discuss examples of corporate that have used corporate communication effectively to build a positive image of the company.

20

Rural Marketing Communications

20

Rural Marketing Communications

Seventy per cent of our population lives in rural India. This percentage is becoming lower because of factors including urbanisations, literacy, opportunities in other growing sectors such as services, etc. Urbanisation/Migration are expected to see the rural population reduced to less than 60 per cent by 2025.

Former US ambassador to India, Galbraith had this to say about Indian villages: It is there that one finds "dignity of life."

The Past

Rural India has been the focus in the country's five year plans. Mammoth river valley projects, fertiliser factories, canals and irrigation facilities, rural electrification, literacy, connectivity through roads, development through Block Development Offices, crop research, high yielding breeds (hybrids), biotechnology, etc., are transforming the lives of villages.

Rural India has always had its own word of mouth communications. Such interpersonal communications are even today common at the village well, groups of villagers going together early in the mornings to the river or tank, the temple, the village meeting place, social occasions, festivals and so on. Newspapers are read by the literate persons but to a group. The transistor radio is a common durable, continuously listened to by the villager.

The learned from the city pass on information about the 'latest' to the villagers. After the World War II was over, in Punjab and Haryana, the army men (retired) formed themselves as 'drum beaters' and went around in their regalia but as a medium for commercial products. Sandwich boys going round big villages were common.

There are also markets such as the weekly **shandi** and the stalls put up at thousands of melas, temple festivals etc.

There has always been demand for some products in rural India. However, such a demand was not universal for all these products.

While cloth, jewellery etc., were universally needed, items such as gripe mixture, barley powder and the like were in demand only in certain parts.

In the early 1950s, rural market began attracting the attention of several organisations. Geoffrey Manners, for example, had organised different tiers of sales personnel. From the better off in cities, there were sales personnel who traveled by bicycle or the local camel/ bullock/donkey/horse cart into villages. Similarly, goods were also transported in all forms of vehicles. Manners also pioneered obtaining the drug license (the relevant category for selling aspirin) in order to extend the channels to even paan shops.

Several organisations such as Burmah-Shell, Wimco, Tatas (for Dalda), Reckitt and Colman (this became Hindustan Lever much later) were all into rural marketing. The new media these organisations introduced included the rural publicity van equipped with 8 mm projectors. Rural cinema houses in South India were also used. Mela participation was popular. Some organisations such as Liptons tried tinplates, using film stars as models. However, the rural audience thought the tinplate announced a new film, for they could not read any way. Another instance was an insurance advertisement with a group seated on a Rajasthani type of ornamental bed. The audience in Bengal did not relate, stating the advertisement was for some other strange people. The Insurance company changed this into the **charpai** used in Punjab along with turbaned villagers common there and in other northern areas. **Charpai** in Bengal was associated with carrying the dead and once again the advertisement failed.

All these companies, however, used the **melas** and in particular the bigger melas like Sonepur, Nauchandi, the Kulu Dasara fair etc., with success.

The "wholesalers" (for example in Burra Bazar in Calcutta) bought the goods and either sent their representative by train or other means of transport to deliver or the village dealer came to the big town to procure his needs. The efforts of the publicity vans and films were not at that time linked to creating distribution chains, but to educate the local dealers that they should add the item to their list of procurement.

The Market

There are over 6,25,000 villages in our country. Population-wise, the break up is roughly thus:

Population	% of total
10,000 +	0.24
5,000 to 9,999	0.85
2,999 to 4,999	6.25
1,000 to 1,999	14.23
500 to 999	23.10
200 to 499	29.27
199 or less	26.03

Age-wise, 61% of the population are between 15 and 59, the target market for most goods. Literacy levels are distorted in the sense, Kerala and Mizoram have the highest while the average, which was 23% in 2001 is slowly increasing.

It should also be noted that whereas in Kerala there is no dividing line between two villages–everything is contiguous there, in Rajasthan, the distances between villages are fairly large. Hilly areas present a different picture. Thanks to plentiful water, Punjab is very rich and the quality of life of an average villager there is different from elsewhere.

Rural electrification is 100% in Tamil Nadu and power outages are less there. On the other hand, several other states that boast of fair degree of rural electrification have power outages between 10 and 18 hours in rural areas.

There are "rich" areas such as Kaira, the Headquarters of AMUL, an outstanding example of cooperative venture. This has been followed by many other cooperatives, such as Lijjat Pappad. There are parched poor areas too elsewhere. While agriculture is the main occupation, in coastal villages, it is fishing. Occupations too change from place to place.

Out of the 1,52,786 post offices in our country, 89% are rural. Our country has had the Green and White revolutions that transformed us into a grains exporting country besides making us the world's largest producer of milk.

Rural women have been found to be motivators and more responsible than men. Women managed credit banks help them to become self-employed. Many women organisations have developed in rural India, where traditional additional employment was through rolling **agarbathis, beedis,** handicrafts etc. The Khadi and Village Industries are also focusing on rural cottage/small industry development.

Rural share of the market for various products is reckoned as follows:

Percentage of Rural Household Consuming the Products

Product	Percentage
Soap, talc etc.	25
Lipsticks, rouges	13
Textile products, ready mades	30
Silks	60
Woolens	53
Consumer durables	30

In recent times, in just two years in the late 1970s, volume of sales of detergent cakes in rural India jumped 160% and of tea 45%. Thus the rural sector indicates a fairly large chunk of the total Indian market for non-agricultural products:

Rural India is also the largest buyer/user of transistor radios and battery operated cassette players.

This achievement is because organisations that have been investing in rural marketing since the early 1950s could solve their transportation, warehousing and channel problems and also develop the needed human resources. Organisations like the Lever Group (including HLL, Brooke Bond, Lipton,Kissan, Ponds etc.), ITC, and others have been pioneers—along with the (face unknown) marketers of **beedis**, betel nut powder, tooth powder, etc., who could be "locals." The marketing organisations behind betel nut, tobacco, snuff, **sheekakai** powder etc., used paper packaging and the quantities were small. Such packaging happens to be the forerunners of the sachet/foil packs introduced first by a cough mixture maker and soon followed by the giants in order to reach the buyers of small quantities.

The above observations do not include items such as seeds, fertilisers, pesticides, pump sets and other related items including cement, Government promoted solar cookers and the like. Mostly, these are bought through easy bank loans (besides being subsidised) and through the village cooperatives.

Estimates indicate that there are over 20,00,000 retail outlets (other than textiles) in rural India. There are primary rural markets, the shandi markets and meals and fairs. On an average up to 75 families are served by one outlet. These outlets are village cooperatives, fair price shops, private dealers (largest segment) and the weekly **shandis**.

Levers/Liptons are reported to have developed 40 to 50 C&F agents, close to 4,000 stockists in feeder towns and reach over six lakh selling outlets. Some 1,200 field sales staff, besides those of the dealers, cover the markets regularly.

Drawbacks: There are ready road and street maps of towns. Such a facility for villages is just not there for the planner.

The capability of television is a reach of 99% of the population but without electrification or affordability, the reach of this medium is limited.

Media

There are two aspects of rural India. Over 60% of rural India is not exposed to what we call organised media. However, it is a fact that nearly 70% of the cinema revenue is from cinema houses located in rural places. In South India, there are "touring" cinema houses which relocate to another place every six months.

The transistor radio is very popular. The All India Radio (Akashvani) regularly researches the rural programmes and what is needed is to choose the correct rural radio broadcasting stations and programmes to reach out.

Cassette players are equally popular. There are at least 40,000 **melas** and fairs and festivals worth looking at. There are syndicated publicity vans (for communications only) besides the company's own sales-cum-publicity vans.

Wall paintings, stenciling on walls etc., banners and the like are also popular.

There are animal drawn vehicles, painted on both sides with advertisements, carrying battery operated loudspeakers or megaphones. Announcements are made, leaflets are distributed.

Folk media such as street theatre, **harikathas**, magicians and the like are also effective. Now that the Panchayati Raj is a fact of life, it is being used for societal problems too. The Government of India has a song and dance division as well as rural exhibitions division. These operate to a fixed schedule and purpose.

Many organisations operate rural publicity-cum-sales vans. These are equipped with audiovisual equipment, roll-down tents, generator etc. Normally, these choose a **shandi** market. A day earlier, the van goes round several villages in the area and where crowds can be gathered, shows audio-visuals, undertakes demonstrations and also sells. On the **shandi** day, since crowds gather there, there is continuous screening to sets of audience, demonstration and sales. Innovative games/contests are also organised to make the audience brand conscious.

Rural India can become brand conscious, if only efforts are there, and in fact almost one hundred per cent of the toilet soaps sold there today are known urban brands.

The planning of rural communications is related to the distribution channels and coverage. The communication expert needs to personally visit the places and then decide on the media mix.

Special Addition

The Highway Market

One development in 2006 was the attention given to national highways. The petrol/diesel filling stations are already being re-engineered to look modern, have more facilities including toilets, shops etc. The areas of their location will be turned into what is, in the West, called "service" areas. Such areas will have food courts, rest room facilities and shopping facilities. The shopping part is reckoned at several hundred crores of rupees and organisations such as Arvind Mills, Foodworld etc., are said to be considering investing in this market.

It should be noted that these are in "rural" India and therefore form part of rural marketing, but segmented—to cater to the long distance travellers.

The audience is the long distance traveler from one city to another, already covered by mass media advertising. The spin off would be that these outlets will attract nearby villagers to visit these modern shopping facilities. The advertising here will be restricted to sign boards, hoardings and the discounts offered.

Summary

The rural communication has challenges due to a target which has a different cultural and educational profile as compared to urban consumers. Also media availability for rural consumers is limited. This calls for innovative communication media. Events such as melas, fairs and festivals can be used for promotional activity.

Keywords

- Rural marketing communication
- Rural India
- Urbanisation

Discussion Question

1. Discuss the challenges of rural communication.

21

Marketing Communications: Going Global

21

Marketing Communications: Going Global

In India, we do get many overseas television channels such as HBO, news channels including BBC, CNN and also cartoon channels, fashion, animal planet, travel etc. These carry advertising for global brands and Indian advertisers such as Oberoi Hotel who have properties in other countries, Kerala Tourism etc., also use some of these channels globally.

In going global, it is vital to understand the differences between the countries—and in particular the society, its values, customs, lifestyles, beliefs. We also need to know the government regulations, approvals for certain type of products and other regulations.

It is advisable to also find out business practices and financial arrangements—how assured would be payment.

One floor polish maker of the US entered the Japanese market but found nil sales despite fairly heavy advertising. The reason: the smell of this polish was no different from the smell of the toilet cleaner used by the local people. The polish changed its smell but after heavy and avoidable expense.

Another organisation tried to sell its American size food product. Again, failure. In Japan, because of shortage of space, homes are compact and refrigerators are small. This organisation made the product available in packs to suit the Japanese refrigerator. Again, at avoidable wasted expense.

Fig. 21.1: International Celebrity – International Brand

In Italy an American organisation tried to sell a corn product as breakfast food. However, to the citizens, that corn was a feed for pigs!

We have so far witnessed global brands in India: Philips, Sony, Prestige Samsung, LG and several makes of cars such as Honda, Hyundai, Ford, Volvo etc. (some like Enfield exist in India but not in the country of origin).

There are some aspects we are probably aware of, such as in the US, the driving is on the right of the road while in the UK it is left. In Israel, blue colour is associated with death like black is associated in many other countries. In the Arab world, Urdu, Persian, etc., are written left to right and in Japan/China their script could be written top down too.

In Japan (as in many Eastern countries) sitting cross legged is a mark of insult. (All over the world, for shoe and shoe polish advertising, cross legged poses work, but not in Japan.) Also, when exchanging a visiting card, if one places it in a wallet and keep the wallet in the hip packet, it is an insult: the Oriental takes it that is the place you give to that person. On the other hand, if the card be put in the breast packet, it is an honour. These aspects of cultural values must be learnt to avoid showing wrong advertisements on television or in print advertising.

Indian companies have now started global branding: Videocon, Mahindras etc., have already made a mark. Several garment makers are opening up in overseas markets. Tatas are entering the car market with Indica and other makes. Earlier, the IT companies such as TCS, Wipro, HCL went global.

Our Airlines operate flights globally. Sizeable (Indian) ethnic population lives overseas. Indian TV channels and also local channels catering to Indian population do an effective job. Local print media aimed at ethnic groups are also available.

In developing marketing communications, "local" expertise is a must. We in India are more filmi and use music and jingles. Similarly, there are peculiarities in each country. As an example, for a consumer product, the Japanese agency recommended to an American advertiser that cartoon style should be used. The advertiser was first aghast but was persuaded by the agency and that style worked.

The foregoing are guidelines and this is not an exhaustive and in depth lesson.

Summary

While planning for global communication we have to keep in mind differences in culture, political environment etc. While we can promote global brand, the communication has to be customised due to the differences mentioned earlier.

Keywords

- Global brands
- Global communication

Discussion Question

1. Discuss why communication in global market needs a different focus.

22

Marketing Communications for Not for Profit

22

Marketing Communications for Not for Profit

The title of this chapter can as well be "Social Marketing Communications." In all societies and especially in ours, which has a great tradition, the gains of development have to flow to and shared by people at large. While on one hand there has been a great knowledge and communications explosion, on the other there is poverty, unemployment, population explosion, disease and more.

One of the marvels of the last two decades or so is the technological developments—in IT in particular—that have shrunk the world. Today we are instantly aware of global, national, regional, local problems. Apart from the unforeseen tsunamis, earthquakes, floods and droughts and diseases, we also have problems of gender equation, child labour, evils of dowry, drink and smoking, etc.

All these social problems are, in truth:

- Non-commercial
- Non-profit
- Non-partisan
- Non-political
- Non-sectarian

By resorting to marketing techniques and marketing communications, could these problems be minimised or totally resolved? The answer is YES.

For a start, as in product marketing and communications, in social marketing too, the emphasis is on getting facts by employing research. When undertaking research, the objectives should be:

Fig. 22.1: An illustration of "Advertising for not for Profit"

(i) To identify the ideas that will benefit the society if they are implemented.

(ii) To help in developing distribution and communication programmes in order to effectively cater to the ideas.

(iii) To help in meeting the infrastructure needs.

In almost every country, the government spearheads social welfare —in several areas—be it prevention of floods, health care, disaster management, relief from calamities etc., and welfare schemes. There are other organisations too that are closely and fully involved with social marketing – to mention a few, World Health Organisation, UNICEF, CARE, Red Cross, CRY, hundreds of NGOs, the FPAI, Indian Cancer Society, and service clubs such as the Rotary, Lions, Jaycees, OXFAM and so on. There are also organisations that are devoted to blood donation, eye donation, children's care, old age care, with the Sisters of Charity (Mother Teresa's) as an outstanding example, and more. Today, there are many bodies to create awareness and provide relief in the area of AIDS/HIV alone.

Elsewhere in the world, from around 1960, marketing approach to social problems has been on the increase. As defined by Philip Kotler, Social Marketing is "societally responsible marketing, which calls for four considerations in marketing decision making", namely:

- Consumer Wants
- Consumer Interest
- Society Requirements
- Social Welfare

Social marketing has a combination of different economic and social values behind its motivational base. It is also complex since the requirement is to handle both economic costs and social costs not for profit but for the benefit of the society as a whole. If we have a better society, it is the nation as a whole that gains. A healthier population means more productivity. A well-informed society means better values of life and so on.

In order to be meaningful, social marketing must take into consideration, the cultural and religious background as also beliefs/ customs of the people. We need to involve the people so as to overcome barriers to successful communications before launching any project. Without people participating actively, no problem can be solved. Successful social marketing would—and this should be accepted by the people—help the individual serve himself and thus the society at large.

In a developing country such as ours, the problems that we face are enormous. Ideally, we need to segregate and prioritise these.

Then we need to classify these as: (i) Those that need continuous attention, (ii) Those that need attention for a specified period of time and (iii) those that could be taken up at a later time. We also need to plan for calamities—the tsunami, the Bhopal tragedy, the rain havoc in Mumbai, the earthquakes, the floods and heavy rains in South India—all happened and could again happen without any warning at all. We need a crisis management team and volunteer corps.

For each one of our problems, marketing parameters need to be applied:

(a) Identification of the problem in all its dimensions.

(b) Identification of the solution, after evaluating all alternatives.

(c) Identification of the benefits that will accrue.

(d) Identification of the target audience, describing them in terms of age, sex, location, educational level, occupation, life style and more.

(e) Identification of other people (and groups) and associations who could influence the target audience. These could be religious leaders, peers, film and sports icons and so on.

(f) Identification of cultural, traditional and religious values and practices.

(g) Identification of barriers to successful communications.

(h) Organising and maintaining a reach programme—a distribution system and experts who would be available to solve any problems—say if it is a planting season, who could arrange seeds and other inputs on time—who will guide in choosing the right species to suit the specific soil and condition. The answers mean added value to the audience.

(i) Study of media availability and reach. In so doing, recognise the role of communications and, if used, how would be integrated with other efforts.

(j) Establishing management and operating plans, with a feedback system.

The main stress firstly, in social marketing communications, is to try and create awareness, impart knowledge in such a way that it leads to a need. Secondly, this need has to be converted into an urgent want. When this is achieved, there is participative action by the people, which results in the success of the project and in a way of life.

A good example could be quote from a presentation by K. Kurien:

> "Many cases of cancer can be cured if the disease is detected early. It was found that a large number of patients went too late, practically in the terminal stage to the hospital."
>
> In the Tata Memorial Cancer Hospital, in 1979, there were four free cancer check-up clinics. The problem was to persuade patients to go for early checks. If this is done, the cure rate would improve and there would be less waste of resources.
>
> An advertising agency donated its expertise. It undertook research using a sample of 600 literate adults from different income groups from 12 different localities. Even at the mention of cancer, 49% of the respondents showed fear. They associated cancer with certain death, as incurable, as a dangerous disease and something terrible.

The overall findings revealed very high awareness of cancer as a disease but very poor awareness of causes, symptoms and treatment. Very few believed cancer could be cured.

Communications were then designed to combat ignorance and to bring a change in attitudes. This was a highly successful campaign.

Most social workers and leaders are earnest and committed people. Where they can err is in their consciousness. For them, stating a case is adequate. They cannot imagine or bear to be rejected. They do not necessarily change behaviour or attitude of people, who distort the message to suit their convenience. However, when the same people are trained and marketing principles taught, it enables communications to try and influence by:

(i) Activating latent attitudes.

(ii) Overcoming resistance by presenting facts against ignorance.

(iii) Facilitating existing behaviour patterns.

(iv) Focusing attention on an emotional need.

(v) Selectively reinforcing the attitude against another attitude.

(vi) Promoting HOPE and not fear.

In most developed countries, voluntary organisations have been set up to undertake social advertising. Experts in various disciplines contribute their time and resources, free of cost and in a dedicated manner. Some of these organisations are:

- The Advertising Council, the US, UK and Japan and other countries.
- The World Wild Life Fund
- UNICEF.

In Singapore, the Peoples' Association helps in the implementation of social marketing projects. In our own country, when condoms were first launched in the early 1960s, marketing organisations such as Wimco, ITC, Brooke Bond, Lever etc., volunteered services and their distribution system in the distribution of condoms.

The International Advertising Association, India chapter has been endeavouring to launch an organisation like the Advertising Council and if this is formed, there could be remarkable improvement in our communications in social marketing.

Related Subject: Fund Raising

Not for profit organisations need funding—besides grants they may be getting on a committed basis. This they get by appealing, organising events, creating and marketing items such as calendars, greeting cards, Walks, sponsored events like a film stars meet etc., for the good cause—with the result many leading commercial organisations—as a policy—extend support.

Summary

Today communication, particularly advertising is being used extensively for non-commercial purposes. Polio eradication, prevention of AIDS, drug abuse, child marriage, duty of citizens during elections, eye/organ donation, responsible behaviour as a driver on the road are some of the issues tackled by this kind of communication. UNICEF, Red Cross are some of the other institutions involved in these areas.

Keyword

- Social marketing

Discussion Question

1. Discuss some of the major campaigns used for non-profit projects.

23

Advertising and the Brand

23

Advertising and the Brand

The Brand

The dictionary tells us that brand means searing the skin with a mark as a sign of ownership. Although this is associated with cattle (those who have seen Western movies would understand this readily), in reality it started with slaves being branded by the Caucasian owners. With the slaves, it was ownership and with cattle later on, this became a system of trademark.

In our own country if we look at packaging and advertising of up to the late 1950s, goods were associated with "Trade Mark" and not brand. With the advent of marketing in the 1960s, brand gradually replaced trademark.

Ask yourself: Why do more people consume a specific brand of chewing gum or chocolate or a particular brand of aerated water? Why is it that a manufacturer of refrigerators by different names (only the label changes) find that only one of his brands commands the market? Why is it that one brand of Japanese brand of TV made by the same manufacturer for a British brand find that the former is sold at a much higher price and is the market leader?

Why is it that the term photo-copying or photo-stating not used and instead, Xeroxing is used and has become generic and synonymous with copying?

In marketing communications, the brand name is one of the most powerful tools and the selection of the right brand name is intricate.

Some people point out to a factor called K. This is the first consonant in Indian languages and the crow of course caws Kaa Kaa. Cook or look or Coke or knock, all have the k sound. Why did Kellogs choose K? Or a chocolate called Kit Kat?

The unwritten rule behind a name is—a company's name should not exceed 10 to 15 letters. Why is this so? We are overloaded with information and the market place is like a war theatre, bombarded with more and more products/brands. The brain remembers short names—hence International Business Machines becomes IBM or India Tobacco Company becomes ITC so that people immediately recall. A product name should not have more than four syllables.

The mission of marketing communications is to promote brand-consumer relationships, create competitive differential advantages, build unassailable brand personality and loyal customers. The key to modern branding, therefore, is identification. As other characteristics —because of economic and social development—such as race, religion, sex, etc., get blurred, people tend to identify themselves with what they buy and where they buy.

Brands have pervaded our lives too. Holidays (like sugar or rice) have become a generic product and the sub-products include beach or hill station—with the name of the place that has become a brand. Thus Disneyland is a fun place, nothing like Goa for a beach holiday, tranquil holiday in God's own country: Kerala; the little Asia is either Singapore or Malaysia and so on.

A country too can be a brand. If it is engineering goods, Germany is associated with dependable quality. If it is electronic goods, it is Japan. If it is a flower like jasmine, it is Egypt. If it is sandal, it is India. Taking this route, California promoted the state as a brand and products made there carried the line, "A quality product of California" be it oranges or cheese or whatever. California priced its product little higher because of perceived quality differential.

Today, in the real marketplace, shoppers think of themselves in terms of choices they make. Brand is part of today's lifestyle.

Names are hard to come by. Good names are so limited in number that several organisations register thousands of names for a diverse list of product categories. Some, who have a good and successful brand name, register alternative names which can otherwise be used by competition—an **agarbati** manufacturer, for example, has a brand—let us call it Natya Rani—has registered all forms of dancing from ballet to Manipuri as his brands.

Some names, when transliterated into another language may carry a different connotation. Thus, Bobby when written in Tamil would read Paapi or Sinner.

The selection of a good brand name should be based on:

(i) Connotation
(ii) Benefits perceived
(iii) Positioning
(iv) Acceptability in a specific cultural environment
(v) Legally permitted or otherwise
(vi) Competitive brands and their strengths/weaknesses
(vii) Type of packaging

The name should be easy to pronounce as otherwise recall will be difficult. The name, in today's environment, needs to be short too. It should sound pleasant. The association of the name must be good and without any negative ones.

The name chosen could be neutral or identify itself with

(i) A product description
(ii) A product position
(iii) An indirect/arbitrary association with the product itself

Among these, in today's context, positioning and type of packaging are corollaries to the brand name.

Several brand names, not necessarily scientifically chosen, have endured for over a century. Amrutanjan, Lifebuoy and Mysore Sandal all come to mind as brands with over a hundred years of good market shares.

In earlier days, there were not many brands. A brand could be called Waterbury's Compound or Monkey Brand Black Tooth Powder. The market was not crowded and people led lives of more leisure. Today it is a different world and we need to be more scientific in our approach.

The name should be unique. In particular, for a totally new product, which would be the market leader and first of its kind, the name needs to be unique. Also, if a new product would affect the image of the company, it could be given a new name so as to keep it apart from its other products.

Generating brand names should be done by following the criteria. As a first exercise, people should jot down all names that occur to them. Then from the list, eliminate the negative ones, names that are close or similar to competition etc. Then form a short list and thereafter prioritise the names chosen in the order of merit. After this they should follow two simultaneous exercises:

(i) Test all the names with associations, images, perceptions. If need be, add more names. Keep on testing.

(ii) Simultaneously begin a search at the Trademarks registry. As pointed out earlier, many names are registered by leading companies though not used. If names chosen are not available, the exercise should be repeated.

There are regulations behind a brand. Some common names cannot be registered. For example, Total as such may not be eligible for registration as a trademark. However, the lettering style, the colour scheme etc., can be registered. In highly crowded markets such as agarbati, vests etc., this is commonly resorted to.

The mission of a brand name should be to build itself as an asset. With successful brands, line extension becomes that much easier. Where the owners restrict their product lines but yet are market leaders, others pay them a royalty for using the famous brand name for their (not at all competitive) product. Thus, a cigarette company paid heavily for using the name of a Lighter for one of its brands of high priced cigarettes.

There are also occasions where other companies acquire competitive/sick units. In the luggage business, this has happened via merger and in a perfumery business, just for three good brand names, another company acquired a unit, whose proprietor opted out of business.

Establishing a Brand

A brand gets established through the process of awareness, brand recognition, trial, preference, repetitive purchase and use, brand insistence and loyalty.

To the customer, a brand means protection. He trusts his brand and gets value satisfaction and not thinks it a risk. He buys his brand wherever he goes and also talks about it. When a large number of customers behave in the same way as a group, the brand becomes established and as an asset.

To the seller, branding helps develop customer franchise, besides improving the image of his company and protection against infringements. It also ensures uniform quality, improvements in product, better price and an unassailable competitive differential when all products are identical.

Brand Management

Brand Management is a top management responsibility. It is not really a new branch of study and has been practised all the time. In today's changed world of up to the second information via the IT revolution, in a world where stake holders look for more returns per share, the demands on marketing are on the raise. Also, there is the aspect of citizens interests, especially in the area of ecology and environment. This calls for great caution on the part of the brand owners.

The fact that no one can crystal gaze the place of a new brand should be borne in mind. Therefore, brand management applies to existing brands, mostly successful ones.

Since brands are assets, this could also be termed asset management. Also, since every activity today is a product—even a holiday, it is also activity management.

The main functions of brand management are (i) Protect and improve market share, (ii) Improve profits—a trusted brand can have a premium price, and (iii) create assets.

One multinational is in the areas of edible oils, consumer products, toiletries, beverages, foods and more. Elsewhere in the world, because of possible reprisals ecologically and environmentally on the overall functions, the principals of this company sized down the number of products—for a while at a loss. This organisation looks long term on its brand management.

In India, in the 1950s (at that time it was 100% British owned) Reckitt & Colman sold the same polish under three different brand names: Cherry Blossom, Parrot and Cobra. It also had a fourth name Nugget, which was not used. Each of the three brands had regional leadership positions. Parrot, because the tin used more colours, and so also Cobra, were not that profitable as Cherry Blossom. The name association—apart from may be shine—with Parrot (imitator) and Cobra (a poisonous variety of snake) was not flattering. Taking these into account, the management decided that over a stipulated number of years, Cherry Blossom should take over from the other two brands and also be the market leader.

An MNC had been trying to enter the toothpaste market but never succeeded. It had the financial strength not to give up until it came out with a seven letter name and promotion used the same appeal as that of the leader, namely, freshness of the mouth—and this made an impact. The new brand got a good market share. Ciba had a toothpaste Cibaca, which had a decent market share. The company was taken over but there were problems regarding the use of Cibaca as a name. The name was changed to Binaca. However, the owners decided to discontinue toothpastes from their portfolio. This is also brand management.

There has been a marked change in the way people sell products. The entrepreneur offers franchise and thus we have chain stores, pizzas, textiles, etc. Another enterprise decides to have its products made to its specifications by private suppliers. This is very common in readymade garments and knitwear. Tirupur in South India makes different brands of knitwear for the brand owners round the world but to their designs and specifications. So does Ludhiana for woolen knitwear. Bangalore makes jeans (and the maker gets part of his job done in Bellary, another part elsewhere and so on.) This is also common in appliances, food products including biscuits etc.

There are situations that happen because of innovative technology. In the late 1980s, the sachet pack was introduced for a variety of products. Multinationals also introduced this pack for two reasons: (i) to prevent small brands eating into their market, and (ii) reach low income groups who usually buy loose quantities.

An icecream manufacturer in the US (now bought over by Levers) found that different pack sizes/shapes were required for different markets as were the flavours.

Ford had announced (and this is a continuing quote too) that their car could be bought in any colour so long as it was black. Very soon, they had to introduce different colours.

In all these, particularly in franchised areas, it is very important to keep uniform worldwide image. Therefore there is total control on marketing communications.

What this all amounts to is that Brand Management is really the business of top management which can use marketing inputs and methodologies.

The Logo

Take a cardboard box that can contain a computer. Copy three letters I, B and M, the same way the organisation IBM writes them. You now have, not just a box but something that has great value! What you have done is to copy the IBM logo. IBM stands for International Business Machines but the name of the company too has been changed to IBM. One would find companies using short version of their names as the logo in preference to a brand, for the name itself is the brand. Sometimes, as in the case of Indian Airlines, a stylised IA acronym for the full name used along with the full name—IA Indian Airlines. In December of 2005, a new logo was adopted by this Airline while changing the name itself to one word, "Indian". The airline merged and became Air India. In others an extra element is used, as in the case of Life Insurance Corporation of India along with folded (protecting) hands holding a light.

A logo, in the strictest sense, is single piece of type chosen as badge of organisation and used in advertisements, letterheads and so on. It can also be said to be a seal or the initial.

The P logo of Pierre Cardin is used to single the dress apart from others. MacDonald uses an arched m to be different from all the Scottish Macs and regular m typefaces.

However, today, the short name or full name of the company is set in a specific font and the whole, also with the shorter version, is called logo. The font is chosen to reflect the character of the company: Lakme for example is elegant and thin to denote femininity. Air India shows dependability and flight. Tata Steel shows strength and dependability. Same goes for ACC cement. Company logos are registered for their exclusive use.

Logos form part of the packaging and so do mascots these days. A mascot is another element like the character Gattu for Asian Paints not used now, the Maharaja was originally developed for use on in-flight stationery in Hong Kong and when this was found popular, used in other marketing communications of Air India.

All these are mnemonics, that is, devices to aid memory.

The logo, brand, trade mark and mascots or mnemonics are also called symbols. In marketing communications, the brand "Cycle" is shown with the text "The symbol of quality". For another product, kumkum, it is the Gopuram, which is called the mark of quality. The words are added to reinforce the use of the mnemonic.

All these have the same purpose: to add to impact, to reinforce the brand image, to foster loyalty and to create immediate recognition— by itself or by association. Thus, the Amul girl is by itself recognised for Amul butter, the Maharaja (a mascot) stands for Air India and the examples are many.

Many of the logos are used in the corporate identity programmes of the organisation, that is on stationery, visiting cards, vehicles, uniforms, packaging, signs, in fact everywhere. Thus, if one were to look at any airlines, one would see the logo plus name on tickets, boarding cards, baggage tags, signs, surface transports, aircraft, menu card, uniforms, advertising etc.

To further stand out, the logo and name also are given distinct colour schemes. IA for example used orange and black. This was chosen because orange colour was a holy and auspicious colour of India and more than anything, its visibility is very long. One can identify an IA aircraft five miles up in the sky.

However, in using logos in corporate identity programmes, there are many musts. Since the usage is wide and includes local procurement at all kinds of places, developed and not developed, it is important that the font used is one that is universally available. Then, the colour: paints are needed differently for painting on metal and walls. Printing inks are also varied. The specifications should be such that these are available universally. Similarly, paper used depends on local availability. This aspect needs to be taken into account.

Usage-wise, the logo must be reproducible in its smallest version on a visiting card and as a large sign over the factory roof. It should be capable of being used in colour/black and white. It should be such that reproduction by stenciling on a jute bag should be as effective as getting this printed through the best offset process or screen process. Above all, it should be as simple as possible.

The Packaging

Some of the best packaged products are "Nature" made. The egg, the coconut, etc., which keep the product inside safe and fresh (for a period of time) are ready examples.

The basic function of packaging is to keep the "content"—intact (Factory Fresh)—be it bulk quantities of say rice or a pouch of betel nut that is retailed. Packaging of industrial products is done to prevent breakages, keeping the product protected against weather or transit damages—since these are sent as cargo by road, sea or air and sometimes it could take months and also during storage.

Packaging of consumer products begins with:

(i) Protection

(ii) Preservation

Apart from these two factors, packaging must have 'barrier' properties: for example, a shampoo in a pouch should not leak. The barrier would extend to prevent contamination, that is bacteria entering the product, to preventing loss through evaporation in the case of liquid or gas and also provide "breathing" if the product is like seeds or live chicken, etc.

Packaging should be leak-proof, hygienic.

The packaging must be product friendly. There should be no chemical properties in the packaging, which would spoil the product properties or colour or taste and so on. The packaging material used must be compatible with the product. It should protect its contents from itself and should do so for several months. The packaging must be eco-friendly. This is of growing importance for now and the future of our world. Packaging must also lend itself to easy and economical transportation. It must be pilfer proof. It should be user friendly and convenient to handle. For medical products, packaging must also be child safe. Rigid quality standards should be observed and maintained. Most importantly, packaging must be convenient for the consumer to use.

Like the brand name, the package must be distinct, stand apart and prominently from the crowd of other products in the shelves. Its shelf appeal is of paramount importance.

Keeping all these into reckoning, packaging should be an item of continuous research from several points of view:

(i) For existing products

(ii) As part of new product research

(iii) As part of product marketing strategy

(iv) For corporate communications

(v) As link between one product and another in a line of products.

(vi) To be aware of new packaging ideas/packaging technology/ packaging materials development and the like.

These do not need any explanation. But for sachets, smaller versions of existing products would not have been made available. But for new material and technology, tea (dip) bags would not have emerged. Technology includes caps for medical products—something that keeps it child safe.

As part of marketing communications—particularly to create renewed interest for established products—new packaging is often times helpful. It is thus common to see a favourite brand to announce "Now in a new pack." For products such as soaps, the shape of the product is also considered under packaging.

Work on the packaging must be begun as soon as the product concept itself has been finalised. The product must "position" itself. If a product has to spell "class" the company should not scrimp and must set specifications that are compatible with that image.

Some of the low outlay products sell in high volumes. These products are the targets of imitators and fakes. In the marketplace these are called 'duplicates' and sold at very low prices because, apart from the outer packaging, there is no quality inside. Packaging should take care of this problem. Some people do wonder at the lengths to which some manufacturers go to add value to their packaging—such as embossing the brand name, cellophane wrapping the pack and so on. However much their profits are squeezed because of the extra expense on packaging, they have no alternative to innovations —the imitator just cannot afford the extra costs—to protect their quality image.

Innovations are powerful marketing tools. The convenience of pop-top was introduced in canned beer/soda in the US a few years ago. In just 12 months, the brand of beer that had used the pop top attained a 40% share of the market for pop-top packs.

Product application research and therefore convenience to the customer has seen change in product formulation technology or in packaging some products—the best example are deodorants. It started with jars, turned into sticks, from sticks to sprays, to squeeze bottles and then to roll-on shapes. Roll-on is what is popular as anti-perspirent but for rooms it is now aerosols.

Carton/Label

What a customer sees in a shop is the outer pack such as a carton, tin, a label on a bottle or printed plastic containers, or stenciled clothing—in different packaging material. Each of these need to be designed with care.The colour scheme, the quality of material used, the printing and finally the total appearance—together all help in making the product stand out.

Label

For many products, the label is the source for the customer to obtain more and authentic information. Some of the information could also be mandatory—such as batch number, expiry date etc., in medicines or a slogan on a cigarette pack "Smoking is injurious to health." Some need to carry more information on how to treat a reaction—as in the case of chemicals and some on how to handle.

A label must have necessary information such as brand name, manufacturer's name, nature of the product, composition, quantity, life, cautions if needed, maximum retail price, dosage (in case of medicines), etc. Since enquiries can gauge consumer reactions and in some cases help in building customer database, a toll free number is also given.

A warranty is added in the case of some products and this is mentioned on the label.

The amount of information on a label will depend upon the product and the user. While for products such as perfumes very little information is needed or given, in the case of pharmaceuticals, in addition to the label, product information literature would also be part of the packaging.

Merchandising

The packaging should also lend itself as a merchandising tool. In sales promotion exercises, multiple packs, banded packs, more quantity for the same price, enclosing a gift etc., are resorted to and all these are done through the packaging. To sum up, a good package should offer protection, should keep contents safe, lend itself to promotion, be customer-friendly, be informative, be environment-friendly.

Summary

Brand name is one of the most powerful tools in marketing of products and services. Selection of right brand name is an intricate process.

The mission of marketing communication is to promote brand consumer relationships, create comparative differential advantage, build unavailable brand and create loyal customers. The key to modern branding, therefore is identification.

In the past we have seen branding of toothpastes, cosmetics, cars etc. However today, commodities such as salt, sugar and rice are being branded.

Logos and mascots are symbols used to associate a brand with them. Their usage makes brand recall easy. Some of the popular mascots used are Air India Maharaja, Wipro's Sunflower, Onida's Devil etc.

Keywords

- Mascots
- Logos
- Merchandising
- Packaging

Discussion Question

1. 'Brands are key to marketing success.' Discuss.

24

Measuring Advertising Effectiveness

24

Measuring Advertising Effectiveness

The Budget

We have gone through the process of planning the marketing communications and now take up the most crucial element: How much should be spent wisely to achieve the objectives?

Organisations have a Capital Budget and a Revenue Budget. Out of the Revenue Budget, the cost of marketing communications, forming part of the overall marketing costs is decided.

Money spent on marketing communications is a battle for the consumers' money and brand loyalty. Before deciding on a budget, it should be realised that in today's environment the customer is bombarded with too much competing information. This kind of "overload" of information tends to make the consumer indifferent. He could well be satisfied with the brand he uses or one, which was correctly positioned to his segment. He could also be one who goes to the Internet to find out and judge for himself the best option.

Depending on the tasks before marketing communications the brand (and its competition too) may take an attacking or defending or a midway position.

The main criteria for the top management in allocating expenses would, in the final analysis, be:

(i) Profitability or Return On Investment (ROI)
(ii) Market Share

These among other things the management may decide upon.

Both profit and market share obviously are related to the product life cycle and to quote George S. Dayer:

> "During the rapid growth stage, purchase patterns and distribution channels are fluid. Market shares can be increased at a relatively low cost by capturing a disproportionate share of incremental sales, especially where sales come from new users rather than heaviest usage by existing users.
>
> By contrast, the keynote during the maturity stage swings to stability and inertia in distribution and purchasing relationships. A substantial growth in share will come at the expense of another brand, and will be resisted vigorously. As a result, gaining the market share is both time-consuming and costly."

Apart from the product life cycle, we take into reckoning all factors including consumer life cycle and, most important, the long-term objectives of the organisation and the product. Other aspects to be considered will include:

(i) Barriers to entry

(ii) Cyclicity of sales

(iii) Capacity utilisation by the product

(iv) Sensitive aspects: pricing, season, others like sales promotion, service levels etc.

(v) Extent of "captive" business (loyalty)

(vi) Nature of technology: mature or volatile or complex

(vii) Availability of production/process opportunities

(viii) Social, legal, government, union, consumer group pressures, etc.

(ix) Opportunities

(x) Others

The responsibility of drawing up a budget would be that of the person who manages the marketing communications function in the organisation. He would be a two-in-one expert:

(i) Expert in marketing communications

(ii) A businessman, interested in ROI.

How much should the budget be? Is there a formula?

It is difficult to measure the effect of expenses on marketing communications, particularly advertising. However, evidence shows that given a sound product and a sound plan, when the proportion of selling cost on advertising increases, sales revenue also increases, bringing down the cost in terms of percentage of sales.

The earlier chapters took us through the planning of advertising, beginning with the situation analysis and taking us through various facets of advertising—positioning down to strategies. All these are termed the "Task Method" for a budget to be sanctioned.

However, there are other methods in vogue, particularly used by the board level management and/or financial management of the organisation. These include:

(i) The Affordable Method

This method prioritises all budgets under the revenue account and takes into account cash flows and other aspects.

What the CEO or his nominee "thinks" as affordable for the company would become the budget. He may also release the budget in installments—quarterly, monthly and so on.

This method implies that, for each occasion, a "case" would have to be made but the main consideration would never be marketing needs but affordability. This is an un-sound method and has built-in delays too. This method is popular in government and public sector undertakings, where the finance director would hold the powers to sanction or not.

(ii) Percentage of Past Sales

A fixed percentage of the value of past sales (either the year that has ended or an average of the past three to five years) is allotted as the budget to the marketing department, including marketing communications.

The advantage is that the budget is known as a specific amount. No expertise is needed and there is no need to make a case.

On the other hand, there are disadvantages: How will the marketing head allocate between other inputs and marketing communications? Since there is no flexibility, what will happen if there is a sudden need to step up marketing communication efforts by pumping in more money? How will cost escalations for media etc., be taken care of?

(iii) Match the Leader/Competition

This is a copycat method. This is also totally illogical. Whatever the main competitor or leader does is replicated—in terms of scale of marketing communications (creatives could be different but size, duration, frequency etc., would be identical). Cost-wise this is not an affordable method nor will it deliver unless at least the turnover matches the competition. In any event, there is no logic in imitating.

(iv) Fixed Percentage of Projected Sales

By far this method is what is followed by most modern organisations, because this appears to be somewhat more logical. This allows the organisation to look long term and spend far more than sales in the first phases—as an investment, and thereafter—over a period of time—recover the investments and also keep the budget at a reasonable ratio to sales. This also allows for reviews periodically, even monthly, and make adjustments as warranted by the changing situations. Particularly where the attitude is one of investment and research shows this is not going right, the organisation can reduce or stop further expenditure.

For established products, depending upon the product life cycle and other factors, this will be decided on facts, including inflation, cost escalations etc.

(v) Leaky Bucket Method

This follows a bucket filled with water and a faucet somewhere closer to the bottom (which we shall call the danger level) and even if the faucet is kept open, there will always be some water left. If water is replaced with cash and it flows out of the faucet, the flow will stop once the faucet is closed or it can at best not exceed the level at which no flow is possible. The theory here is the bucket is full and at the launch stage the expenses will be heavy and the faucet is closed at a reasonable level. When there is danger by not spending, the tap is opened a little and closed when the need is fulfilled. This exercise is repeated until the bucket is near empty. At that stage, the option is to refill the bucket.

This method is used for new launches or for products that sell only when advertised and the impact lasts for a while.

(vi) Other Methods

Economist model: This uses marginal analysis, marginal contributions in the hierarchy scale of consumer, leading to the best profit orientation and not long-term presence.

Computer simulation model: Several inputs/strategies/alternatives are fed and options obtained. These are studied and the best option adopted.

In reality, however, whatever model is used, the ultimate budget is decided on the basis of a combination of two parameters, namely:

(a) Cost of achieving the marketing communications objectives
(b) How much can the organization afford

Financing of Marketing Communications

In the annual accounts, advertising, publicity, public relations, promotion, entertainment etc., are together called APSP or advertising and sales promotion expenses. These expenses are exempt from tax even though the income tax officials can question and disallow some of the expenses.

Despite this heading called APSP, some organisations absorb some expenses under other heads. Certain companies keep all printing—even of calendars, literature, annual reports etc. under "printing and stationery" head. Some keep market research under R&D! While the stakeholder may not be able to ascertain the actual expenditure on marketing communications, the person in charge of this function would be keeping proper records.

For financing, while financial institutions do give loans for projects, raw material, machinery, working capital etc., very few would offer financing for APSP aspects. In fact, many flatly refuse and consider this as a big risk. This could be an inhibiting factor for the small entrepreneur who may come out with a brilliant product. On the other hand, large established organisations have the leverage and liberty of cannibalising budgets of other products for one which may need extra funds.

Can Marketing Communications Be A Capital Expenditure?

The taxation acts provide and it is also easy to write off all marketing communications expenses at one go each year. While this is so in practice, there is, according to the expert, Joel Dean, a strong case to consider the question, "Can marketing communications expenses be a capital expenditure?"

Dean argues that marketing communications is a business investment for the immediate as well as long-term future. He submits that it may be possible to quantify the efforts needed and returns expected and also the risks involved. Notionally, several organisations do their annual investment planning, which includes marketing communications efforts. However, the planning for marketing communications is under the revenue head. Dean's theory is of academic interest but needs serious consideration.

What are Marketing Communications Expenses?

What expenses relate to marketing efforts? The professionals have made three lists—called white, grey and black.

The white certainly is a legitimate marketing communications expense. The grey depends on whether the expense related to marketing or public relations or other heads and the black is certainly not a marketing expense.

White list

Cost of space in print media, point of sale, outdoor advertising, window displays, store signs, novelties, booklets, advertising directories, yellow pages, stickers on cartons etc., during promotions, dealer bulletins, cinema, TV, radio advertising, production costs related to all these and other legitimate marketing communications.

Costs of modelling, photography etc., subsidies or cooperative advertising with dealers etc., salaries, allowances including administration, conference expenses, travel relating to marketing communications.

Black List

Free goods, packaging development, price list (which is mandatory), visiting cards, house journals, annual reports, advertising for personnel, tenders, annual give aways, greeting cards, etc., are not part of marketing communications.

Grey List

Cost of sampling, demos, participation in expos (exhibitions), painting messages on company vehicles, membership to professional organisations, marketing research, portfolio to sales staff, training, etc.

If these relate to marketing communications, costs go to white list; otherwise (**e.g.,** for promotion of corporate image etc.,) the costs go to Black list.

Evaluation/Research

Evaluation

Marketing communications is, of course, all the time, evaluated through research. However, most research is quantitative while some such as psychographics deals with qualitative aspects.

In evaluating marketing communications four broad issues need to be considered:

(i) Clear understanding of what the problems are and how the research findings will be put to use.

(ii) Once the research project is completed, the researcher does not get to know the use to which it has been put to. The researcher must, however, know. This should be ensured.

(iii) Research is not the end all. It should help in judgment of strategy.

(iv) Performance is normally monitored without checking out whether research inputs have been in terms of decisions taken earlier.

Towards evaluation, we need to use research. Such research—going back to what we have studied so far, needs to be related to the tasks set for marketing communications, not sales.

In any event, research can offer explanations and neither solutions nor predictions. It just cannot equal decision—making. Just consider some situations: The City of Las Vegas in the US—research would have established everything against building that city in the middle of nowhere in the desert. Yet, today it is a success story. Or, take Disneyland in Orlando—once a swamp, unfriendly place. Today it is a big money spinner and one of the "musts" for the tourists. Or, for that matter, would Disney have ventured into animation and created one of the world's most famous icons, The Mickey Mouse?

The Blunder of the Last Century: Around 1985, Coca Cola—because the product was very "Old" over a hundred years old, in fact, undertook extensive improved product tests as well as packaging tests. Convinced that everything was right, the new Coke was launched. What the people who briefed the research organisation and researchers had overlooked was "Coca Cola was part of the American culture" and when the new product was launched, there were protest marches by thousand of consumers.

Coke had the good sense to bring back the original Coca Cola under the name "Classic." One another finding was that there were heavy users of Coke—who formed the culture and there were light users and the research had not given weightage on the basis of usage; instead, it was 'one man one vote' treatment.

Let us look at what an international research guru said in the World Advertising Congress, Tokyo in 1984:

(i) How do you decide which advertising is truly effective? In short and/or long term? How do you cope with the variables that go into the marketing of a product such as sales promotion, merchandising, brand name, pricing etc., as also the advertisement in detail: copy, media used, size, position, etc.?

(ii) Advertisers would like to know, in advance, if their campaign is more or less likely to produce results sought.

(iii) Looking at your advertising strategy, what needs to be done is measure how consumers feel about your brand and competitive brands on a continuous basis.

(iv) Accurate measurement of advertising effectiveness calls for specific advertising objectives, which are defined precisely enough—so that research can be designed to measure these effectively.

(v) There is no substitute for 'facts' and if facts are accurate, free of errors, they could be easily validated.

Marketing Communications Research

Most research studies in the area of marketing communications are quantitative, together with diverse tables and relate to:

(i) Media

(ii) Pre-testing of concepts, advertisements etc.

(iii) Post-testing of concepts, advertisements, meanings etc.

(iv) Comprehensive research of all aspects of marketing communications, including package, price, display etc.

(v) Message research

(vi) Money research

(vii) Colour vs black and white

(viii) Position—special/solus/island/right top of page/others etc.

All these are generally stated but actual research is undertaken based on the objectives set for marketing communications.

Media

In our country, we have research studies such as the national readership survey (this includes viewership/listenership etc., too) of media. In addition, there are studies such as the national applied economic research on demographics, which includes media habits. There are other studies—some on a monthly reporting basis, useful for broadcast advertising in particular. Special studies on other media such as rural, exhibitions etc., are commissioned by the advertiser. Media's own studies such as the ones done by Doordarshan and Akashvani on audience for various programmes are also available.

Pre-Testing

Headline, copy, illustration, concept, tunes, jingles, story etc., are tested for effectiveness etc. This research can be straight, projective whereby pieces and not the whole are shown—as also words and situations to get the response. This test can ascertain association, construction, completion. In this test respondents say what is the first thing which comes up in their minds.They construct a story based on the illustration-situation shown and complete a slogan or a statement.

There are technological means such as the eye camera, which studies the movement of the eyes upon seeing say a colour, a package, headline etc., and where there is impact, the eye focuses for just that longer.

Post-Testing

Post-testing is conducted once the first advertisement is published and then continuously until the campaign gets over, media by media, to assess the success as related to the objectives set.

Money

The limitations imposed by a tight budget which may not have allowed more frequencies or larger sizes or adequate coverage etc., are studied, in relation to objectives so that corrections can be made if the organisation could afford more investments.

Research in General

The definition of research would probably read like this:

> **A careful, systematic, patient study and investigation in some fields of knowledge, undertaken to establish facts or principles.**

In research on marketing communications, the steps to be considered would be:

(i) Define the problem.

(ii) Review what is known about the problem.

(iii) Decide on the research methodology to be used.

(iv) Conduct the research.

(v) Analyse the data.

(vi) Interpret the results.

The research approach is scientific and has distinguishing characteristics, such as:

(a) **Explicity of procedures:** Results and methodology used for obtaining them are described with such clarity that another research expert can read and replicate the same procedure if he so wants. This calls for 100% honesty.

(b) **Objectivity in data collection:** Once procedures are accepted, the researcher must follow them implicitly, even if data/report do not agree with his pre-conceived notion of the outcome. This calls for an open mind.

(c) **Findings must be replicable:** If another researcher were to use the same procedures, the conclusions he would arrive at must be the same.

(d) **Approach:** The approach should be 'systematic' and 'cumulative'. In addition to investigating immediate problems, research aims at throwing up whole bodies of knowledge, all based on evidence.

(e) **Purpose:** The eventual purpose while based on what really happened, should focus on why and how with explanations, control and lead to better understanding.

The research methodology would include several ingredients starting from defining the dependent variable, data collection, response, sample size, design of the study, timings of the study, independent variables, research environment and more. The actual conduct of research will ensure continuous monitoring and the analysis should —as indicated earlier—be qualitative and find out reasons since marketing communications research deals with consumer behaviour more than any other.

Summary

Money spent on advertising is like money spent on other resources like machinery, building, technology, etc. The business is concerned with generating adequate ROI from the money invested in advertising.

Like all other expense activities the process of budgeting is also relevant in advertising. Budget tells us how much money is available for spending.

There are several methods of deciding on the advertising budget. Some of the important budget preparation options are listed as:

(i) The affordable budget

(ii) Percentage of past sales

(iii) Match the leader/competition

(iv) Fixed percentage of projected sales

(v) Leaky bucket method

(vi) Other methods like Economists Model, Computer Simulation Method

One of the debates going on is can marketing communications be a capital expenditure.

The other question that needs to be answered is what constitutes a marketing expense.

Evaluation of marketing communication programme can be done through research. Success of a new brand launch can be assessed by checking market share say after one year. The content effectiveness of an advertisement copy can be checked through recall studies.

Keywords

- Budget
- Market Communications

Discussion Question

1. 'Advertising expenditure should be treated as capital expenditure.' Discuss.

25

Event Management

25

Event Management

Sponsors are an important part of any event. There are numerous event that would not take place without the support of their sponsors. There is a glaring statistic that comes to light as it relates to featuring your sponsors. When people visit an event website they are not interested in who's sponsoring Your event. Sponsorship is the one of the last things the average visitor deems important. As per page views statistics from an event website. The sponsorship page accounted for less than 2% of total page views over a 12 month period.

Beyond sponsorship logos on your event site you need to go beyond just featuring sponsors on your event website. The process starts with trying to find sponsors that your target market actually cares about. Look at the demographics and psychographics of your target market. Can you find a good link between potential sponsors and your target market? Instead of just featuring your sponsors include them as part of your marketing. Include sponsor coupons that your target market can redeem before or after your event. Make sure that sponsors track coupon use. It will not be difficult for you to find sponsors for your event if you are providing your sponsors a definitive Return On Investment (ROI). Using a coupon is one of the easiest ways to show a direct ROI.

In our country, patronage to arts and other causes are part of our history. In every sphere of activity, be it building a place of worship, a park, an educational institution, games like cricket, art galleries, performing arts, poetry, stage... name it, and we have had royal and the rich person patronage.

From an organisations viewpoint, one can describe sponsorship as corporate giving for noble causes such as scholarships, relief funds, etc.

Along the way, before we attained Independence, it was common for merchants to sponsor temple festivals (like the 10-day long spring one). In these, it was common to see the name of sponsor: XYZ Beedis—sponsors of this shamiana and the like.

Today the marketing communications aspect looks at sponsorship as a means to get ROI. In fact, this is an area of public relations and has grown so fast that it has branched out into a separate industry of specialisation.

What is sponsorship? The Howell report (UK 1983) was perhaps the first attempt in defining sponsorship, thus:

> "The support of a sport, sports events, sports organisations or competition by an outside body or person for the mutual benefit of both parties."

(In the US, sports stadiums and teams are owned even by corporations, which get great mileage and make profits—even though this activity is not germane to the field of their work.)

The Howell definition, however, was considered too narrow and in the same year, another definition was suggested by Meenaugham, thus:

> "The provision of assistance, either financial or in kind to an activity by a commercial organisation for the purpose of achieving commercial objectives."

This definition is found loaded and limited to commercial activities. Therefore, more attempts at an acceptable definition followed, including one by **The Economist** of London, in 1986.

This (focused on only sports) is the most accepted version and reads thus:

> "Commercial sponsorship is an investment in cash or in kind—in an activity—in return for access to the exploitable commercial potential associated with the activity."

In today's world, there are both commercial and philanthropic sponsorship. However, in the area of marketing communications, we need to concentrate on the former.

Another aspect of the world of today is the proliferation of television as this medium is emerging as a prestigious one. We have more of sponsorship over this medium than any other. Reasons are: (i) impact on a scale not matched by any other medium, (ii) coverage —if it is a Crorepati or ODI/20-20 matches in India or Who wants to be a millionaire or Baseball in America,or soccer all over Europe, the audience covered is at its maximum; (iii) Prestige. There are disadvantages though (i) High cost, (ii) Since this is a 24 hour medium, temporary nature of the message, and (iii) high mortality of commercials, which tend to bore with repetition.

Today, sponsorship/event management covers a wide number of activities:

(i) Beauty shows.

(ii) Film awards: In these, earlier there was one or two, today the number of awards—in different categories by different channels —is on the rise.

(iii) Feature films

(iv) Sports

(v) News

(vi) Religion

(vii) Health

(viii) Food

(ix) Art

(x) Almost everything else

It should be noted that each of these is also an event and a sponsored programme over television. Some like classical music create the opportunity to have icons as invitees. In some cases, such as a foreign artiste performing in India, although sponsored, gate money is charged and the sponsors even make a profit!

Using This Medium

Ensure that a study is done and choose the best events that have better "association" with the product/service side by side with maximum exposure among the "target audience." If one can afford it, exclusivity should be ensured so that there are no competing messages beamed. Ensure all marketing activities are coordinated in such a way that full advantage can be taken of the sponsorship.

Do's

(i) As in the case of media/strategies, the function of sponsorship needs to be clearly outlined and stated.

(ii) Use of this medium must be integral to overall marketing communications.

(iii) This should be supported by other media activities in strategic terms and not in tactical terms. For example, in the Allahabad Kumbh Mela, a tea manufacturer sponsored facilities through which he also advertised. He ensured that his brand of tea was vended all over—as an integral part of the exercise.

(iv) Choice of event should be related to target audience.

(v) The event must be complementary to both the organisation and the product.

(vi) Nothing should go wrong in implementation. Specialist management of the event is a must.

(vii) The impact and residual effects should be studied.

Ethics: The ethics of sponsorship is being questioned by public interest lobbies—in particular, there is criticism of cigarettes/liquor brands sponsoring events. Here, these companies promote another product—like sports wear, mineral water and the like—with the same brand name (surrogate promotion).

Summary

Event sponsorship has taken an important place in promoting a brand. Sponsorship not only benefits the advertiser but also the event organizers in making the event affordable to the masses for viewing. Of course, care should be taken in choosing an event to match the viewer profile with the brand user profile.

Keywords

- Event management
- Sponsors
- Patronage
- Commercial sponsorship
- Philanthropic sponsorship

Discussion Question

1. List some of the popular events and the strategy of the brands which have sponsored these events.

26

Regulation in Advertising

26

Regulation in Advertising

1. Consumer Protection

The concept of Consumer Protection started with Great Britain's Sale of Goods Act, 1893. This Act reversed the then prevailing **Caveat Emptor** (Buyer Beware) attitude.

The modern consumer protection actions took place in the United States of America. Ralph Nader devoted his full time to the task of consumer protection. This resulted in John F. Kennedy giving impetus to his Bill of Human Rights, 1962. This Bill gave rights to the consumers and includes:

Fig. 26.1: The helpless consumer

(i) Safety
(ii) Be informed
(iii) Choice
(iv) To be heard
(v) Basic needs
(vi) Healthy environment
(vii) Education
(viii) Representation

This Bill became a reality in March 1964 and following this, the 15th of March every year is observed as the World Consumer Day.

Two decades later, the United Nations passed and adopted Guidelines on Consumer Protection on 7 April, 1985 and this has been accepted by almost all member nations.

India: Following the UN guidelines, India passed the Consumer Protection Act in 1986. This provides for the creation of Consumer Councils at the Centre and in every State/Union Territory—and in each State/UT in every District and at lower levels too.

These councils are enjoined to promote and protect consumer rights, which include:

(i) Right to protection against the marketing of goods hazardous to life and property.
(ii) Right to be informed about quality, quantity, potency, purity, standard and price of goods (this is against unfair trade practices).
(iii) Right to be assured, whenever possible, access to a variety of goods at competitive prices.
(iv) Right to be heard and to be assured that consumer's interest will receive due consideration.
(v) Right for redressal against unfair trade practices and/or unscrupulous exploitation.
(vi) Right to consumer education.

Section 9 of the Consumer Protection Act, 1986, provides for creation of Consumer Dispute Redressal Agencies—(CDRAs)—at three levels, namely:

(i) Consumer Disputes Redressal Forum at District level

(ii) Consumer Disputes Redressal Commission at the State level

(iii) Consumer Disputes Redressal Commission at the National level

2. Consumer Movements

At the international level, an International Organisation of Consumer Union (IOCU) was formed in 1960. This has 169 member groups in over 50 countries and four main networks:

(i) IBFAN, or International Baby Food Action network with a hundred plus groups in 64 countries.

(ii) HAI, or Health Action International with 120 groups.

(iii) AGHAST or Action Group to Halt Advertising and Sponsoring of tobacco.

(iv) PAN, or Pesticides Action Network with 300 groups.

The IOCU's objective is to build and provide forceful global response to the power of the advertisers and in particular that of the multinationals.

India: In India we have had consumer protection movements since the 1950s. Our country has no less than 350 consumer organisations. In February 1991, an apex body known as the Confederation of Indian Consumer Organisations was formed with New Delhi as its headquarters, and with its objective to ensure full and effective implementation of the Consumer Protection Act, extending its scope to rural consumers too.

The consumer protection activists, be it a Bahuguna or a Medha Patkar, are dedicated activists and many have professionals as members. They have close national and international links for quick information exchange. They also have good media relations—the responsible media everywhere are for the common man—involve themselves with noteworthy causes and spend their own financial resources too.

The consumer movement in India has slowly and in sustained way developed and is becoming a force to reckon with.

3. Ethics in Marketing Communications

Voluntary efforts: Being "highly visible," marketing communications has been labelled as 'insidious, 'manipulative,' and so on.

To these criticisms, advertisers summarise their point of view as "Marketing communications constitutes freedom of expression" and, if an organisation is licensed to make and market a product, it should have the same freedom to marketing communications also.

Nevertheless, ethics in marketing and marketing communications have been promoted by the advertisers themselves as is evident from the formation of "The Fair Trade Practice" (voluntary body) and the International Chambers of Commerce revising its code of advertising practice of 1937 to restate that

"All advertising should be legal, decent, honest, truthful".

In the 1950s, the Indian Society of Advertisers tried to bring out a Code. It formed a new body called the Indian Advertising Council. In 1956, the ISA brought out a draft code but the Advertising Council did not materialise. Instead, the Indian Society of Advertisers succeeded in establishing the Council for Fair Business Practices in 1980.

In the late 1970s and early 1980s, the International Advertising Association took a new initiative and with the cooperation of all interests—media, advertisers, etc.,—ushered in the Advertising Standards Council of India, (ASCI). This not for profit, self-regulatory body was finally incorporated in 1986 and has been very active. All the complaints are investigated and acted upon/resolved.

4. The Law/Regulations

There are several Acts/Regulations concerning marketing communications, such as:

(i) MRTP or the Monopolies Restriction of Trade Practices Act of 1984.

(ii) The Drug and Magic Remedies (Objectionable Advertisements) Act of 1954.

(iii) The Weights and Measures (Enforcement) Act by each state in India.

(iv) The Emblems and Names (Prevention of Improper Use) Act of 1950.

(v) The Copyright Act, 1957 and amendments from time to time.

(vi) The Prohibition (Alcohol) Acts by some states.

(vii) Drugs and Cosmetics Act of 1940 with provisions for Unani/ Ayurveda etc.

(viii) The Trade Mark and Merchandise Marks Act of 1958.

Codes laid down by bodies like:

(a) Indian Newspaper Society.

(b) Doordarshan.

(c) Akashvani.

(d) Cable TV Network (Regulation).

(e) Tobacco.

(f) Right to Information.

(g) And many more, including amendments to many of the above Acts.

Public Perception of Marketing Communications/ Advertising and Culture/Meaning Transfer

1. Public Perception of Marketing Communications

How does the public and especially consumers, view marketing communications? In the United States of America, two independent researchers, Rena Barton and Theodore F. Dunn undertook a study under the supervision of academicians of the Universities of New York, Columbia, North Carolina and Harvard Business School. This study was done in 1980s at the request of the AAAA or American Advertising Agencies Association. An independent sub-committee of AAAA implemented this study.

Questions for which answers were sought included:

(i) Compared to other institutions, how important to the American public is advertising?

(ii) How favourable or unfavourable is the public to advertising?

(iii) How does the public feel about specific elements: social, economic, content, etc., of advertising as a business activity?

The general findings revealed that:

(i) Advertising is not seen by most of the public as a topic of great concern when compared to other aspects of daily life.

(ii) There were no great differences among different classes of people in their reaction to advertising.

(iii) A substantial majority of advertisements noticed by people did not stimulate any strong feelings—either positive or negative.

(iv) Among the few advertisements that did evoke strong feelings, favourable feelings outnumbered negative reactions.

(v) Some kinds of products were likely to get more of negative response than other kinds of products.

Studies in India were undertaken in the 1980s and also later by the Indian Society of Advertisers, by **The Economic Times** and also others who monitored broadcast over television and radio, which revealed:

> "Advertisements were found to be a source of information and very useful. Among TV viewers, advertising commercials were found to be even more entertaining than other programme."

2. Advertising and Culture

Advertising takes the shape of a newspaper layout, a television commercial using a story (story board), a radio spot and so on. Through advertising the cultural fabric of a country could be affected. Or, since advertisements consist of characters who play roles in commercials, the meaning may not be perceived as the advertiser intended.

In 1980, the McBride Commission criticised advertising for its uninvited cultural intervention in the Third World countries. Even earlier to this, in 1970 and 1976, Paulo Faire had observed:

- .... The invaders penetrate the cultural context of another group, in disrespect of the latter's potentialities: they impose their own view of the world upon whose they invade and inhibit the creativity of the invaded by curbing their expression.
- .... For cultural invasion to succeed, it is essential that those invaded become convinced of the intrinsic superiority of the invaders. The value of the latter thereby becomes the pattern of the former.

Creators of advertising tell us that what is sold is part of a lifestyle, not a product. According to them, culture is reflected in people's lifestyles. Is this true? Is it an excuse because of lack of effort to understand or is it sheer indifference/ignorance?

In 1992, in our country, a brand of cigarettes called Jaisalmer was launched. Professional magazines told us that Jaisalmer would be India's Marlboro cigarettes. How wrong one could be is perhaps revealed better in another study, which is as follows:

In Malaysia, two professors, Michael and Cathereine Frith studied culture and advertising. Their findings reveal that advertising played the role of an invader of culture, a foister of an alien culture. The Friths pointed out that:

(i) The practice (and profession) of Advertising originated in the Western social context. The concept is entirely grounded in Western social experience.

(ii) The major advertisers have always been (and continue to be) MNCs. The advertising agencies creating the bulk of advertising in the country of study, both for MNCs and national advertisers, are also MNCs—linked directly or indirectly through former employees who have served such MNCs and are trained in their methodologies.

(iii) The training imparted to employees has been such that they abandon indigenous culture as old fashioned. Instead, they adopt the values taught by their managements. There has been no effort to develop indigenous methods or cultural values in this field.

(iv) The result has been that a hegemonic culture, Western culture, is unconsciously imposed. Such cultural invasion pervades all walks of life of the elite. (In the Indian context, at ADSCAN 1989, Abid Hussain said the same and gave the figure as 200 million Indians as forming the elite class)

The Friths compare the cultural values of different cultures thus:

Cultural Values

Parameter	Eastern Value	Western Value
Discourse	Euphemistic/Indirect	Direct, get to the point straight
Feeling	"We" or group identification with authority figures	Individualistic, vertical or horizontal with class
Decision Making	Collaborative	Hierarchial
Problem solving	Intuitive	Logical
Attitude	Fatalilstic	Deterministic

The Friths then compare two advertising campaigns, one for Marlboro Cigarette and the other for Singapore Airlines. These were exposed in international media with audience from various countries. The Friths applied the three level Dyer's approach to evaluate the campaigns:

Level 1: Primarily the subject matter in totality. In press advertising, this will include colour, size, shape, model used, typography etc.

Level 2: The subject matter such as how the models relate to each other and/or to the product, and to allegories, images etc.

Level 3: Underlying values that reveal the basic attitudes or ideology.

What emerged is as follows:

Marlboro

Level 1: The symbol used is that of a Western culture, the cowboy. He is American, wears a white hat (in almost all the advertisements that is), which symbolises good. The brand name Marlboro is featured prominently and forms, in fact, the focus of the advertisement. The pack also stands out against muted earth tones of the dark background.

Level 2: The cowboy symbolises (allegory) the American dream of freedom from constraints, of wide open space and of man against the elements. This theme runs through American folklore and is preserved and nurtured via literature (cowboy books), films, dress, songs, theme towns/parks etc.

Level 3: The cowboy is alone there by choice, because "individualism" is the very core of American culture.

An additional point: The Marlboro cowboy is always a white man, symbolising male patriarchy and the whites, historically being the ruling class in Western societies.

Singapore Airlines (1980)

Level 1: Two stewardesses, photographed and shown slightly out of focus. One is smiling whilst the other is pouring a drink to a passenger who is seated. Both hostesses are very feminine, dressed in traditional patterned outfits. The colours are soft pastels. Copy, written by hand, adds a personal touch. The viewer senses an invitation to fly with the Singapore girls in the advertisement.

Level 2: Invokes Asian hospitality, symbolised by the two hostesses (allegory).

Level 3: While the Marlboro cowboy is alone, the two hostesses keep company with each other, consonant with the value of collectiveness or group consciousness/feeling, pervasive in most Asian societies.

Additional point: In Asian context, in public, women generally keep company of other women while men gather around other men.

This study by the Friths highlights the cultural facets and also begs the question—Could advertising creativity be culturally relevant and original?

3. Meaning Transfer

In today's scenario, television commercials have the largest audience. Many of these use icons and in any event there is a story outline for every commercial. May be at first the audience accepts the message as promoting a product but with repeated viewing, the mannerism/behaviour of the "stars" imparts the wrong lesson.

Examples: (i) Sachin Tendulkar and his son (in the commercial) walk into a shop, where the kid breaks several items. No worry for Sachin —he has a credit card to settle the bill!

(ii) in a detergent ad, brother and sister walk along when the sister trips in a puddle of dirty water. Brother takes umbrage, jumps crazily in that water, splashing dirt all over. No worry for the mother —the miracle detergent is there! She is not even dismayed at the behaviour.

On the other hand, a kid being dropped by her father to school asks "Whose big car is this?" and the answer is telling. It is her daddy's!

Since commercials keep on changing frequently, it is advisable to watch the latest and judge for oneself. The idea of raising these points is to make the readers aware of the pitfalls. He should develop professional standards and originality.

In the immediate post-Independence years, there were attempts to make advertising more Indian than Western. The sentiments of the people tended towards projecting Indian culture and art.

The wish expressed in 1956 by a film maker and advertising executive of renown, C. Das Gupta to quote "The study of indigenous methods of advertising constitutes—to my mind—one of the basic tasks of Indian advertising today. Perhaps there is too much centralisation in Indian advertising to permit such a local approach to advertising. Convention, convenience and "the law of least resistance" makes us centralize in cities and standardise in English. In this sub-continent, it is much more realistic to administer advertising more and more locally using more and more indigenous methods, with central control only over basic policies..." (**Format**, May 1956).

Children and Advertising

Advertising to children is the act of marketing or advertising of products or Services to children, as defined by national legislation and advertising Standards. Advertising to children is often the subject of debate, relating to the alleged influence on children's consumption. Rules on advertising to children have largely evolved in recent years. In most countries, advertising for children is now framed by a mix of legislation and advertising Self-regulation. The following are concluded: Scope and Form

Advertising to children uses traditional media—television, radio and print—as well as new media (internet and other electronic media). Packaging, in-store advertising, event sponsorship and promotions can also be Means to attract children. There is no universal definition of a child (although UNESCO—the United Nations Educational, Scientific and Cultural Organisation, defines early childhood as ages 0–8 years). Children are otherwise defined according to national jurisdictions. For the purposes of advertising law, the definition of a child varies from one jurisdiction to another. However, 12 is commonly used as a cut-off point, on the basis of the widespread academic view that by the age 12 children have developed their behaviour as consumers, effectively recognise advertising and are able to adopt critical attitudes towards it.

There is no global data on ad spending directed at children, only data for specific sectors. However, according to the Federal Trade Commission, food and beverage companies (44 companies reporting to the FTC) in the US spent approximately $1.6 billion in 2006 to promote their products/services to children. In the United Kingdom, Greece, Denmark and Belgium advertising to children is restricted and in Quebec, Sweden and Norway advertising to children under the age of 12 is illegal.

The European Union also has framework legislation in place, which sets down minimum provisions on advertising to children for its 27 member states. The EU Audiovisual Media Services Directive, due to replace the Television Without Frontiers Directive in all member states by the end of 2009, sets out several EU-wide rules on advertising and children:

Advertising shall not cause moral or physical detriment to minors, and shall therefore comply with the following criteria for their protection:

(i) It shall not directly exhort minors to buy a product or a service by exploiting their inexperience or credulity.

(ii) It shall not directly encourage minors to persuade their parents or others to purchase the goods or services being advertised.

(iii) It shall not exploit the special trust minors place in parents, teachers or other persons.

(iv) It shall not unreasonably show minors in dangerous situations in addition:

   (a) Children's programmes may only be interrupted if the scheduled duration is longer than 30 minutes.

   (b) Product placement is not allowed in children's programmes.

   (c) The Member states and the Commission should encourage audiovisual media service providers to develop codes of conduct regarding the advertising of certain foods in children's programmes.

In the United States the Federal Trade Commission studied the issue of advertising to children in the 1970s but decided against regulation.

Advertising Standards

In many countries worldwide, advertising is also governed by self-regulatory codes of conduct. Advertisers, advertising agencies and the media agree on a code of advertising standards—a set of ethical and behavioural rules they commit to respecting—which is enforced by a self-regulatory organisation, often an independent industry-funded body, responsible for drafting, amending and enforcing the code. Self-regulatory organisations for advertising are increasingly following the best practice model agreed with regulators and consumer and public health groups in Europe. At a minimum, the general aim of self-regulatory codes is to ensure that any advertising is 'legal, decent, honest and truthful', but in most countries detailed rules are in place for different advertising techniques and sectors.

Advertising self-regulation is built on different levels. On a global level, the International Chamber of Commerce has drafted a global code on marketing communications. All forms of marketing communications worldwide must conform to the ICC Consolidated Code on Advertising and Marketing. The code includes a specific section, detailing the special care needed when communicating with children.

Since 2006, a global code of practice on food marketing communications is also in place. The Framework for Responsible Food and Non-Alcoholic Beverage Marketing Communications of the International Chamber of Commerce (ICC) sets down global requirements for food and beverage marketing communications on all media, including the internet Key provisions include: the need for substantiation for claims or health benefits; no encouragement of excess consumption; no representation of snacks as meals; no undermining of healthy lifestyle messages; no undermining of the role of parents.

These codes provide a minimum requirement for marketing communications worldwide. National self-regulatory codes, based on the ICC codes, are established, policed and enforced by local Self-Regulatory Organisations (SROs) and industry in over 100 countries and apply to a range of media, increasingly also including digital marketing communications. The ICC and national codes are reviewed regularly to ensure that they remain relevant to local, cultural and consumer concerns and that they promote best practice. The ICC Framework is applicable globally but is a minimum standard designed to be adapted and transposed into SR codes at national level. Many countries have implemented SR provisions that use the ICC Framework as a basis, but go further in several respects, depending on local considerations. Examples include Australia, Brazil, Canada, Chile, France, Ireland, The Netherlands, New Zealand, Spain, the UK and the US.

In addition to industry-wide self-regulation, individual companies and industry sectors have introduced a wide range of additional provisions relating to marketing communications directed at children. For example, most multinational food and beverage companies have developed their own policies on food and beverage marketing communications to children and, most recently, have announced the joint implementation of these individual commitments.

In July 2007, 10 of these companies (now 13) announced a common pledge in the US—the Children's Food and Beverage Advertising Initiative, mirroring a similar initiative by 15 companies in Canada —the Canadian Children's Food & Beverage Advertising Initiative; and followed by 11 companies in Europe with the EU Pledge. Under these initiatives, participating companies will cease advertising to children under 12, other than products that meet specific nutritional guidelines, based on international scientific recommendations. A similar Pledge Programme was launched by leading food companies in Thailand in May 2008 and in Australia in mid-2009.

Media Literacy

Media literacy is a relatively new discipline, aimed at teaching individuals and children in particular to understand and use the media to their advantage. Media literacy is increasingly recognised by governments and international organisations such as the European Union and the World Health Organisation as a key tool to help children understand and deal with today's complex media environment.

MediaSmart is an established media literacy education programme focused on advertising. Launched in November 2002, Media Smart is a non-profit media literacy programme for school children aged 6 to 11 years old. Media Smart develops and provides, free of charge and on request, educational materials to primary schools that teach children to think critically about advertising in the context of their daily lives. MediaSmart materials use real examples of advertising to teach core media literacy skills. MediaSmart is funded by the advertising business in the UK and is supported by the UK government and EU institutions. Since 2002, MediaSmart has been launched in Belgium, Germany, the Netherlands, Finland, Sweden, Portugal and Hungary.

Sex Appeal

The use of overt sexual appeals (mentioned in ealier chapter) in print advertising has increased considerably in contemporary advertising practice. According to an article by Henthorne and LaTour (1994), today it is common for a reader of any age to pick up a general-interest consumer magazine and find an advertisement featuring provocatively posed and attired models for many consumer products. During the past decade, the use of sexual appeals in print advertisement has become commonplace. Among the most memorable companies, which base their advertisement on sexual appeals, is Calvin Klein. Their ads usually feature a nude couple in a somewhat provocative position. Also, many of the print advertisements for Calvin Klein jeans are just as suggestive and memorable. Ads of this type are designed to elicit what the originators hope is a vicarious experience of sensuality.

The use of sexual appeal in advertising continues to be a very controversial topic. A 1994 study done by Henthorne and LaTour revealed that an ad which contains a strong overt sexual appeal results in a significantly less favourable attitude toward the ad, attitude toward the brand, and purchase intention than an ad that contains little or no sexual appeal. For example, a very controversial AXE subway ad in Mexico has an arrow pointing up the shiny miniskirt of a woman driving a convertible sports car. Another ad shows a man with his arm around a woman with the arrow pointing down the front of her low-cut shirt. Next to the arrows is the statement: "To get what you want". In this case, strong overt sexual appeal is being used in order to place brand remembrance on AXE. As a result, the brand also has been labelled as a company which is involved in strong overt sexual advertising. Although the use of highly sexual print ads is viewed more negatively, the attitude of women is significantly more negative than that of their male counterpart. As the morals and ethics of society change over time, what is considered appropriate and acceptable by society must also change. Therefore it is necessary to re-evaluate the assumptions on which strategic decisions are based when it comes to print advertising. Advertisers need to look at potential social issues and consequences at stake when considering an advertisement based on sexual appeal.

Summary

More than any other time consumers are exposed to choice of several brands. Marketers use all kind of strategies to influence consumer behaviour. Some of the practises used by the marketers have been found to be unethical. All over the world governments have tried to curb unethical practises in advertising through regulations. Advertising should be honest, should be self explanatory, and should respect social system.

Keywords

- Regulation
- Insidious
- Right to information
- Hegemonic culture
- Individualistic
- Hierarchical
- Fatalistic
- MediaSmart
- Consumer protection
- Manipulative
- Indigenous culture
- Euphemistic
- Collaborative
- Intuitive
- Deterministic
- Overt sexual appeals
- Consumer dispute redressal agencies/forum

Discussion Question

1. Identify brands which have unethical practices in advertising and explain where they have gone wrong.

27

Influence of Cinema

27

Influence of Cinema

Influence of Cinema in India

The Past

India is the largest producer of feature films in the world. The Hindi and thereafter the Tamil movies have worldwide following and gross large box office collections.

The number of theatres within India, however, is not even. While most of the cinema houses are located in towns with less than one lakh population, the majority of the houses are in South India. In Tamil Nadu, for example, there is a cinema house for every 20,000—and on the assumption there are 21 shows a week/capacity of hall at 1,000, even a newborn child may be a film viewer. The cinema is so powerful that quite a few politicians, including chief ministers, were/are from this industry.

There are also rural cinema houses—particularly in South India. In the tea gardens of Assam, once a week, a van equipped with projection equipment, screens a film to the workers and this is open air.

Cinema houses had always been used for screening slides and these were mostly from "local" dealers. In 1956, advertising films were introduced with success. For a long time, there were powerful distribution companies for advertising films and this medium was used extensively. In the 1980s, however, television took over and the ad film distribution organisations more or less went out of the scene. There are, however, small players who offer screening in a few theatres.

The credit for promoting products via a song, set to a tune that was popular, goes to the late Sri A.V. Meyyappan. In a 1940 film, appropriate to that period, a song talks about the bridegroom-to-be—and asks the bride to be to use Hazeline Snow, a brand of soap, and a brand of talc. He promoted quite a few products as a make-up.

A.R. Rahman, in **Roja,** hit the headlines with his **"Chinna Chinna Asaai,"** a lyric. Nutrine and its agency, Visesh, launched "ASAI" with an adaptation of this song, **"Thinna Thinna Aasai"** and the product was a great success.

Walt Disney succeeded with animated films and followed this with marketing of icons/toys of characters from his films. This became a success and was followed for most films. Later on, in the late 1940s, the number of items increased and Disney stores specialising only in own products are a common sight all over the world. In India, after the serial **Mahabharat** got released, Draupadi sarees were a craze. One spectacle frame worn in a film by an actor became the "style" for teenagers. Perfumes were named after film stars. Films were funded by Coal India, Amul and Singareni Collieries, to name a few. These highlighted the industry. However, none of the actions, except of Disney's could be said to have been planned.

The Transition

Earlier, cinema needed a "studio" in order to build massive "sets" for filming. Then the new technology enabled "outdoor" shooting and this made studios redundant. Then, with the advent of television, the film industry experienced a slump period. Many Hollywood studios were up for sale.

Media itself became an industry. Media barons emerged, owning not only print but also television and radio media. In the meantime, technology made it possible to view films on vcrs, thereafter on CD or DVD and now direct to home etc. Simultaneously, music became a big industry. The media also realised the importance of special areas such as sports as a big money earner.

Technology and "management" of resources has impacted the cost of making films/music/videos etc. By around 2005, the scene had become different. With the use of digital technology, it is reckoned that a feature film could be made for under Rs. 25 lakh. Probably, this excludes the fees of mega stars.

An article in the All India Management Association magazine informed the readers that many corporate giants, such as Reliance and Sahara were investing in feature films. In the meantime, while someone like Ivory Merchant lived and produced films in English language, a new breed of overseas film makers eyed the Indian market and the result has been simultaneous production of films in English in addition to select Indian languages.

The Latest Scene

By 2006, the scene had changed and this industry now encompasses multiple interests such as:

Cinemahouseswithsinglescreen(traditional)	12,000 +
HomeTheatres(ownedprivatelyandsome used commercially	Numberunknownbutmany
Digitalscreentheatres150with3,000more by 2006 end	Many
Multiplex theatres	200with1,500morecoming
Production as TV only screening films	Many
Films for overseas Indians	Many
Filmssubtitled/producedforinternational audience	Many

The new media barons, in addition to entering the film business, are also in the business of cable television, FM radio stations, music (including remixes), CD/DVD sales etc.

At the moment, the attempts (mostly successful) at using the cinema medium comprises promoting products (in use). For example, in Farenheit 9/11 over 50 different products are shown.

On their own, because of usage by the public at large, products like Cycle Agarbati, Amrutanjan, Fevicol etc., are part of the film dialogues and are also shown.

Corporate houses are funding films and have set up their own production houses. The cinema medium offers challenges and the directions for use of theatres.

How intelligently this powerful mass medium is used depends on the strategists, both creative and media.

Summary

From time immemorial advertisers have used cinema as a medium to promote their brands. However, it is during the last decade that an organised effort has been made to place brands in scenes where viewers can see the brand prominently. Leading soft drink brands, and other consumer products have found alternative in cinema advertising.

Case Studies

Case Studies

Case Studies I

Case Study 1: "Everyone has a reason to Pray. Cycle Pure Agarbatis."

The Rangsons Group of Mysore is in diverse fields: electronics, perfumes, floral and herbal extracts, export marketing, incence sticks and more. This case history is restricted to agarbatis and to marketing communications exercises.

"Any weaver can produce a good cotton saree but it takes the best weaver who has the passion and devotion to produce a pure silk bridal saree as only the best in Kancheepuram can do. There is a gulf between the run of the mill and the extraordinary and my agarbati will be pure and extraordinary. I believe in value and quality first."

These are the words of the company's founder, Mr. N. Ranga Rao. Since the agarbati was an offering to the Gods, he also inculcated the spirit that the product should be "perfect" and in crafting agarbatis, there should be devotion and also that profit should be the least motive.

N. Ranga Rao & Sons (NRR for short and the flagship company in the group) forayed into agarbatis in 1948 with a clear resolve "Lead others by innovation and execution." At that time in our country's history, the humble agarbati was another "commodity" dealer-driven for its survival. Agarbatis were in 'generic' fragrances such as rose, sandal, jasmine and so on. The founder introduced many firsts, quickly adopted by others in the industry and these include (a) standard size, (b) burning quality, (c) protective packing, (d) packaging,

(e) branding, (f) exports, and changing the commodity buyers visiting Mysore or Bangalore, (g) marketing in a contemporary and planned manner. The company, unlike any other in this field, established its own Research and Development Laboratory, one of the best in the world and its own specialist marketing organisation: Rangsons Marketing Private Limited. This company is on par with the best marketing organisations in our country. The founder also trained his children and they are acknowledged among the best in the world in the fields of aromatherapy and perfumes. The group has the advantage of NESSO, a leader in floral/herbal extracts.

In tune with the changing tastes and times, the company ventured into another first. Bouquet fragrances in agarbati. After thorough research and testing, a bold approach was initiated. Name the brand, "Cycle Three in One" and introduce a distinct packaging. The reaction to this new concept was very good and other manufacturers were quick to copy this concept by introducing agarbatis as three something or as five in one, seven in one and so on. Even an MNC, Reckitt & Colman came out with their agarbati with the USP that it had pure Ganges water! However, it was the users who gave their verdict—Cycle Three in One was unique and way above others in terms of quality and fragrance.

One aspect of the marketing communications had been engaging the attention of the consumers and this was correct positioning. It took several years with test after test, research followed by research. The parameters for positioning were:

(i) The association must be strong with Cycle Agarbati.

(ii) It should be the truth and nothing but the truth.

(iii) It should be simple.

(iv) It should be creative and not easy for anyone to imitate.

(v) It should empathise.

(vi) It should be capable of building quick acceptance and trust.

(vii) It should have impact.

(viii) It should be easy to promote.

(ix) It should help the communication stand out in the heavy clutter of today.

In a market where there were hundreds of brands, with very little positioning differentiation (all promoted praying followed by other uses), Cycle aimed for a distinct personality. The result:

The positioning statement: Everyone has a reason to pray cycle pure agarbati

Along with adopting this POSITION statement, television commercials were produced to create awareness and impact. Using very carefully selected strategies, marketing communications using TV as primary media along with other media in the mix, Cycle has attained a place in the hearts of consumers.

Note: Cycle is the umbrella brand (with a range under the name Cycle by itself), along with other Cycle brand range such as Lia, Rhythm etc.

(Story Board of TV commercials, Pack, examples of items using the Positioning statement—as many as possible.)

Case Study 2: Live-In Casual Wear

Whenever VIP is mentioned it is invariably linked to Blow Plats luggage manufacturers. There is another VIP, a brand of hosiery from Maxwell Apparells Ltd. better known for innerwear brands such as Frenchie, Bonus, Feelings etc. Mid-nineties hosiery brands of this group had reached a turnover of Rs.200 crore and growth was slow with new entrants like Roopa, Lux, Dixcy etc. Reddy and Path are promoters of these popular brands decided to enter casual wear market to accelerate growth and diversify into this new Greenfield market by launching denim jeans.

Till early 1990s denim jeans were considered to belong to premium category. The brands were priced high, available in restricted cities and outlets. It was late 1990s that Arvind entered the economy segment through Ruf and Tuf, and made denim jeans a mass product. At this time another brand Trigger entered the popular price segment.

VIP commissioned advertising agency Contract to launch their denim jeans. After extensive market research the brand name LIVE-IN was chosen for the denim jeans to be launched by Maxwell group. The agency was asked to work on a communication campaign for LIVE-IN denim jeans. The story board worked on the attitude of youth, the desire to keep on the same jeans day and night. A male model uses the jean to go out, sleeps in it, and finds it so comfortable that does not like to remove it even for washing, but enters the machine with jeans on and comes out still wearing but a pair of clean LIVE-IN jeans. The story board evoked a predictable response from the promoters, **"Ad may chokri nahin hai, brand nahin bikega"** (the ad does not have a girl and hence the brand will not sell.)

All other brands were taking the beaten path of showing scantily dressed girls to promote the brand. The campaign was cleared under reservation, let us give a try. Over a period of time the brand became a leader in the mid segment belying the perception that a female model was required to sell jeans.

Case Study 3: Surrogate Advertising

Oxford Dictionary defines surrogate as substitute. In recent times we have come across a new social phenomenon, surrogate mother or substitute mother.

The same concept has been applied by marketers to promote products which are regulated by government for consumption. Tobacco, alcohol are some examples.

In the Indian context tobacco was the first product to be targeted by government health authorities, public bodies, and international health organisations. There was a ban on on advertising tobacco on select channels like broadcasting. There were no restrictions on print media.

1970s saw another wave in the society in the form of wide spread social drinking. Due to political compulsions, advertising was banned for alcohol. This resulted in manufacturers using surrogate advertising to promote alcohol consumption.

Kingfisher beer promoted as KF mineral water, Directors Special whisky also used the same route of mineral water.

Alcohol is a big business the revenue from various taxes contributes to government revenues. This has become a important Economic activity.

Should government allow products to be manufactured and then restrict their marketing? Should brands used for alcohol be totally disallowed from extension to other product categories to prevent surrogate advertising? Examples:

(i) King fisher beer, Kingfisher mineral water, Kingfisher airlines.

(ii) Wills filter cigarettes, Wills sports wear.

Case Study 4: Deceptive Advertising

The underlying importance of advertising in a market economy is to provide information to consumers and enable them to make appropriate choices in consumption.

Many advertisers give incomplete information, exaggerate claims, over promise under deliver, mislead, threaten the consumer, and create anxiety. Untruthful or deceitful advertising has become order of the day. A advertisement by Singapore airlines offering in bold letters return fare between Bangalore Singapore at Rs.5,999. Just Rs. 6,000 it is cheaper to fly to Singapore than Mumbai.

But there is a catch. On the offered price there is an asterik, which means read further for rider. The rider printed 1/7 th size of the main offer, tucked at the bottom of the copy among other things says that additional taxes of Rs.7,150 has to be paid. The total cash outflow for the traveller for the ticket works out to Rs. 13,149.

This is more than twice the amount shown in the main body of the copy. Sweet deal from SA is no more sweet.

Case Study 5: Success Story of AMUL

Is there anyone in this country who has not seen the Amul ads on the hoardings by the road sides, and not chuckled? The longest running ad, still has not lost its charm with its never-changing famous moppet in polka dotted frock and a half pony tied up.

The slogan has always been 'Utterly Butterly Delicious'. What is it about the Amul ad that has kept the viewers wanting more?

The biggest success seems to be like that of the common man, no particular time or period could have frozen this character. It does not belong to an era. It has moved along with time reacting to the new events through time.

Fig. 1: Amul uses Humour

41 years of Ad campaign

Fig. 2: Another example of Humour by Amul

In 1966, Sylvester DeCanha, who was the managing director of the advertisement agency ASP, got the account for Amul. The country saw the birth of a campaign whose charm has endured fickle public opinion, gimmickry and all else. Eustace Fernandez (the Art Director) and Sylvester decided to create a character that would charm the attention of every house wife in the country. They thought of a little girl and so it came about that the famous Amul Moppet was born. And she has always remained the cute little 4-year-old girl eating butter.

In October that year, in the city of Mumbai on many lamp kiosks and the bus sites the ad of the little moppet on a horse was displayed. The baseline said 'Thorough Bread, Utterly Butterly Delicious Amul'. It was a matter of just a few hours before the daCunha office was ringing with calls. Not just adults, even children were calling up to say how much they had liked the ads. And that was a clear indication of how successful this campaign was going to be.

Conveying a message

Fig. 3: Using Topical News

Through all the events taking place in the country, Amul always had a reply to it. It is up to date with current affairs. The first escalator in Mumbai in 1979 was celebrated with a slogan 'Automatically Amul'. When the city witnessed a power shortage, the Amul girl said 'ta ta power?, Amul, Unlimited Supply'. When the Mumbai police were dealing with underworld don Dawood Ibrahim's sister Haseena Parkar in cases ranging from extortion to cheating and forgery in May this year, the hoarding simply said 'Haseena Maan Jayegi?' In the early 1990s, when the colas were getting popular, the tongue-in-cheek remark was 'Eat the Real Thing'. When the world feared a collapse on Y2K, Amul girl interpreted the phenomenon as 'Yes to Khana'.

The Amul girl, apart from promoting a $1-billion brand, bring smiles to millions. And this smile has spelt huge success and changed the livelihood of over 2.5 million Gujarat farmers. The sales figures of Amul butter have jumped from a few lakh rupees in 1966 to over Rs. 500 crore now. Apart from rapid growth and trustworthiness, the four-year-old girl has also ensured a virtual monopoly for Gujarat Cooperative Milk Marketing Federation Ltd. (GCMMF) that sells Amul brand of dairy products.

In the last four decades, the girl has dealt with all the contemporary issues—be it politics, sports, society, entertainment, art, weather, infrastructure, science or technology. But despite the cut throat competition in FMCG sector, GCMMF is not spending more than Rs. 2 crore on Amul butter advertisements annually on the country's oldest running campaign. The agency, daCunha Communications, which gave a face to brand Amul, does not need to run to the client every time for getting the art work approved. The agency claims that even the top management comes to know about the art work when the advertisement goes on the hoardings.

Fig. 4: Indian Cinema and Amul

From the 1960s to 1990s, the Amul ads have come a long way. While most people agree that the Amul ads were at their peak in the 1980s they still maintain that the Amul ads continue to tease laughter out of them.

Where does Amul's magic actually lie? Many believe that the charm lies in the catchy lines. That we laugh because the humour is what anybody would enjoy. They do not pander to your nationality or certain sentiments. It is pure and simple, everyday fun.

Fig. 4: Popular Cricketer and Amul

The success story of Amul says one thing to all the other ad campaigns that did not manage to last too long or had to get a whole new look in order to stay in the market. Its a mixture of keeping with the times, humour and understanding the need of the hour of the people. Amul boarding are a thing of attractions in India.

Case Study 6: Misleading Advertisements

The concern about companies promoting unhealthy practices is growing. This is visible in advertising targeted at children and young adults. Companies are making aments in responds to complaints by public. Some examples of TV Ads, which have been withdrawn after complaints about the appropriateness.

I.

Company : Neo Sport Broadcast

Product : Neo Sports Channel

Visual : A young boy, spring is to become a big cricketer, is shown wearing cricket gear and playing a shot in the air. He later comes back to his original state with a bucket and broom in has hand.

Complaint : Advertisement encourages child labour, which is banned.

Action : TV commercial withdrawn.

II.

Company	:	ITC
Product	:	sunfeast Biscuits
Agency	:	FCB – Ulka
Visual	:	A young boy attempts to play basketball, is not able to reach the basket and is, therefore, bullied. The mascot of the company gives Sunfeast biscuits to the boy, who after eating it, instantly grows taller and is able to reach basket.
Complaint	:	Visual depiction likely to exploit the vulnerability of children. Ad is misleading.
Action	:	TV commercial withdrawn.

(**Source: Business Today** 26 August 2007)

Appendices

Appendices

Appendix I

Advertising Companies of India

Advertising is a big business in this era in India. Indian Advertising industry has witnessed a prominent globalisation. With the inception of various divisions,the advertising industry has undergone a sea change. Indian consumer's deepening pocket and blooming markets for ad-spends have touched new heights in India. The Indian Advertising Companies are creating stories and brand experiences in a way that engages and involves. The best Indian sites offers the names of the top advertising organisations in India.

Here is a list of the top Indian websites and a quick glance at them will help you to get the required knowledge about the websites.

Top Advertising Companies of India

Ogilvy and Mather

This is one of the leading advertising company in India. This organisation believes that devotion to the brand defines the profile of their company. This company has offices across the globe. The objective of the company is to build brands. It is a subsidiary of WPP Group plc. The headquarter of the company is in New York.

J Walter Thompson India

One of the most popular company in the advertising industry is J Walter Thompson India. Their objective is to make advertising a part of the life of the consumers. This is also world's best advertising brand with about 200 offices in 90 countries. This company is the first one to introduce pioneer careers in ad for women, sex-appeal ads and also produced the first ever sponsored —TV programme.

Mudra Communication Pvt. Ltd

This is one of the renowned advertising company of India. This advertising organisation was founded in the year 1980 at Mumbai. Recently, the Ad company declared the addition of public relations, rural marketing, events etc. The head office of the company is in Mumbai.

FCB-Ulka Advertising Ltd

One of the best companies in India in the advertising arena is FCB-Ulka Advertising Ltd. In the US, this advertising company ranks third and tenth in the world having about 188 offices in 102 countries. Their aim is to reflect the needs of the brand and not the personality of the brand. It has about 500 professionals and no prima donnas.

Rediffusion–DY&R

This advertising company of India has made a benchmark in the field of creativity. India's fifth largest advertising company is Rediffusion. This advertising agency offers a wide array of integrated pr services for external and internal communications. The primary strength of the company lies in the media relations.

McCann-Erickson India Ltd

The prominent name among the best advertising companies of India is McCann-Erickson India Ltd. They define work in relation to the impact that advertising has on the lives of masses. The testimony of the company in which it firmly believes is the campaign of Coca —Cola—'Thanda Matlab Coca Cola'.

RK Swamy/BBDO Advertising Ltd

It maintained the record of remaining consistently among the top 10 advertising agencies in India. Established in 1973, this advertising reached great heights. This is also India's no.1 research company in the market sector and is fully run by Indians. Brand Equity is an integral part of the company.

Grey Worldwide (I) Pvt. Ltd

A significant name in India in the world of advertising agencies is Grey Worldwide (I) Pvt Ltd.The company is primarily based in Mumbai and has offices in Kolkata, Ahmedabad, Bengaluru and New Delhi. It is a subsidiary of Grey Worldwide. The company specialises in advertising and marketing services.

Leo Burnett India Pvt. Ltd

It has a significant presence in about 96 offices in 10 countries. This advertising agency was awarded the 'Worldwide Agency of the Year' in 2004.They are proficient in explaining how a single image is worth thousand words and can break the barriers of language but not at the cost of the ad's emotional power.

Contract Advertising India Ltd

This advertising company of India is one of the leading advertising agencies in India. It is one-to-one customer life cycle management advertising agency. It was founded in 1992 and is situated in Mumbai. It offers a wide range of services like online marketing and strategy and many others.

Appendix II

Top 100 Advertising Compaigns of the Century by Bole Garfield

1. Volkswagen, "**Think Small**", Doyle Dane Bernbach, 1959.
2. Coca-Cola, "**The Pause that Refreshes**", D'Arcy Co., 1929.
3. Marlboro, "**The Marlboro Man**", Leo Burnett Co., 1955.
4. Nike, "**Just do it**", Wieden & Kennedy, 1988.
5. McDonald's, "**You Deserve a Break Today**", Needham, Harper & Steers, 1971.
6. DeBeers, "**A Diamond is Forever**", N.W. Ayer & Son, 1948.
7. Absolut Vodka, "**The Absolut Bottle**", TBWA, 1981.
8. Miller Lite Beer, "**Tastes Great, Less Filling**", McCann-Erickson Worldwide, 1974.
9. Clairol, "**Does She...or Doesn't She?**", Foote, Cone & Belding, 1957.
10. Avis, "**We Try Harder**", Doyle Dane Bernbach, 1963.
11. Federal Express, "**Fast Talker**", Ally & Gargano, 1982.
12. Apple Computer, "**1984**", Chiat/Day, 1984.
13. Alka-Seltzer, Various ads, Jack Tinker & Partners; Doyle Dane Bernbach; Wells Rich, Greene, 1960s, 1970s.
14. Pepsi-Cola, "**Pepsi-Cola Hits the Spot**", Newell-Emmett Co., 1940s.
15. Maxwell House, "**Good to the Last Drop**", Ogilvy, Benson & Mather, 1959.
16. Ivory Soap, "**99 and 44/100% Pure**", Proctor & Gamble Co., 1882.
17. American Express, "**Do You Know Me?**", Ogilvy & Mather, 1975.
18. U.S. Army, "**Be All that You Can Be**", N.W. Ayer & Son, 1981.
19. Anacin, "**Fast, Fast, Fast Relief**", Ted Bates & Co., 1952.
20. Rolling Stone, "**Perception. Reality.**", Fallon McElligott Rice, 1985.
21. Pepsi-Cola, "**The Pepsi Generation**", Batton, Barton, Durstine & Osborn, 1964.

22. Hathaway Shirts, "**The Man in the Hathaway Shirt**", Hewitt, Ogilvy, Benson & Mather, 1951.
23. Burma-Shave, "**Roadside Signs in Verse**", Allen Odell, 1925.
24. Burger King, "**Have it Your Way**", BBDO, 1973.
25. Campbell Soup, "**Mmm mm Good**", BBDO, 1930s.
26. U.S. Forest Service, Smokey the Bear/ "**Only You can Prevent Forest Fires**", Advertising Council/Foote, Cone & Belding.
27. Budweiser, "**This Bud's for You**", D'Arcy Masius Benton & Bowles, 1970s.
28. Maidenform, "**I Dreamed I Went Shopping in My Maidenform Bra**", Norman, Craig & Kunnel, 1949.
29. Victor Talking Machine Co., "**His Master's Voice**", Francis Barraud, 1901.
30. Jordan Motor Car Co., "**Somewhere West of Laramie**", Edward S. (Ned) Jordan, 1923.
31. Woodbury Soap, "**The Skin You Love to Touch**", J. Walter Thompson Co., 1911.
32. Benson & Hedges 100s, "**The Disadvantages**", Wells, Rich, Greene, 1960s.
33. National Biscuit Co., "**Uneeda Biscuits' Boy in Boots**", N.W. Ayer & Son, 1899.
34. Energizer, "**The Energizer Bunny, Chiat/Day**", 1989.
35. Morton Salt, "**When it Rains it Pours**", N.W. Ayer & Son, 1912.
36. Chanel, "**Share the Fantasy**", Doyle Dane Bernbach, 1979.
37. Saturn, "**A Different Kind of Company, A Different Kind of Car**", Hal Riney & Partners, 1989.
38. Crest Toothpaste, "**Look, Ma! No Cavities!**", Benton & Bowles, 1958.
39. M&Ms, "**Melts in Your Mouth, Not in Your Hands**", Ted Bates & Co., 1954.
40. Timex, "**Takes a Licking and Keeps on Ticking**", W.B. Doner & Co & Predecessor Agencies, 1950s.
41. Chevrolet, "**See the USA in Your Chevrolet**", Campbell-Ewald, 1950s.
42. Calvin Klein, "**Know What Comes Between Me and My Calvins? Nothing!**"

43. Reagan for President, **"It's Morning Again in America,"** Tuesday Team, 1984.
44. Winston Cigarettes, **"Winston Tastes Good—Like a Cigarette Should"**, 1954.
45. U.S. School of Music, **"They Laughed When I Sat Down at the Piano, But When I Started to Play!"** Ruthrauff & Ryan, 1925.
46. Camel Cigarettes, **"I'd Walk a Mile for a Camel"**, N. W. Ayer & Son, 1921.
47. Wendy's, **"Where's the Beef?"**, Dancer-Fitzgerald-Sample, 1984.
48. Listerine, **"Always a Bridesmaid, But Never a Bride"**, Lambert & Feasley, 1923.
49. Cadillac, **"The Penalty of Leadership"**, MacManus, John & Adams, 1915.
50. Keep America Beautiful, **"Crying Indian"**, Advertising Council/ Marstellar Inc., 1971.
51. Charmin, **"Please Don't Squeeze the Charmin"**, Benton & Bowles, 1964.
52. Wheaties, **"Breakfast of Champions"**, Blackett-Sample-Hummert, 1930s.
53. Coca-Cola, **"It's the Real Thing"**, McCann-Erickson, 1970.
54. Greyhound, **"It's Such a Comfort to Take the Bus and Leave the Driving to Us"**, Grey Advertising, 1957.
55. Kellogg's Rice Krispies, **"Snap! Crackle! and Pop!"**, Leo Burnett Co., 1940s.
56. Polaroid, **"It's So Simple"**, Doyle Dane Bernbach, 1977.
57. Gillette, **"Look Sharp, Feel Sharp"**, BBDO, 1940s.
58. Levy's Rye Bread, **"You Don't Have to be Jewish to Love Levy's Rye Bread"**, Doyle Dane Bernbach, 1949.
59. Pepsodent, **"You'll Wonder Where the Yellow Went"**, Foote, Cone & Belding, 1956.
60. Lucky Strike Cigarettes, **"Reach for a Lucky Instead of a Sweet"**, Lord & Thomas, 1920s.
61. 7 UP, **"The Uncola"**, J. Walter Thompson, 1970s.
62. Wisk Detergent, **"Ring Around the Collar"**, BBDO, 1968.

63. Sunsweet Prunes, **"Today the Pits, Tomorrow the Wrinkles"**, Freberg Ltd., 1970s.
64. Life Cereal, **"Hey, Mikey"**, Doyle Dane Bernbach, 1972.
65. Hertz, **"Let Hertz Put You in the Driver's Seat"**, Norman, Craig & Kummel, 1961.
66. Foster Grant, **"Who's That Behind Those Foster Grants?"**, Geer, Dubois, 1965.
67. Perdue Chicken, **"It Takes a Tough Man to Make Tender Chicken"**, Scali, McCabe, Sloves, 1971,
68. Hallmark, **"When You Care Enough to Send the Very Best"**, Foote, Cone & Belding, 1930s.
69. Springmaid Sheets, **"A Buck Well Spent"**, In-house, 1948.
70. Queensboro Corp., Jackson Heights Apartment Homes, WEAF, NYC, 1920s.
71. Steinway & Sons, **"The Instrument of the Immortals"**, N.W. Ayer & Sons, 1919.
72. Levi's Jeans, **"501 Blues"**, Foote, Cone & Belding, 1984.
73. Blackglama-Great Lakes Mink, **"What Becomes a Legend Most?"**, Jane Trahey Associates, 1960s.
74. Blue Nun Wine, Stiller & Meara Campaign, Della Famina, Travisano & Partners, 1970s.
75. Hamm's Beer, **"From the Land of Sky Blue Waters"**, Campbell-Mithun, 1950s.
76. Quaker Puffed Wheat, **"Shot from Guns"**, Lord & Thomas, 1920s.
77. ESPN Sports, **"This is SportsCenter"**, Wieden & Kennedy, 1995.
78. Molson Beer, Laughing Couple, Moving & Talking Picture Co., 1980s.
79. California Milk Processor Board, **"Got Milk?"**, 1993.
80. AT&T, **"Reach Out and Touch Someone"**, N.W. Ayer, 1979.
81. Brylcreem, "A Little Dab'll Do Ya", Kenyon & Eckhardt, 1950s.
82. Carling Black Label Beer, **"Hey Mabel, Black Label!"**, Lang, Fisher & Stashower, 1940s.
83. Isuzu, **"Lying Joe Isuzu"**, Della Famina, Travisano & Partners, 1980s.

84. BMW, **"The Ultimate Driving Machine"**, Ammirati & Puris, 1975.
85. Texaco, **"You Can Trust Your Car to the Men who Wear the Star"**, Benton & Bowles, 1940s
86. Coca-Cola, **"Always"**, Creative Artists Agency, 1993.
87. Xerox, **"It's a Miracle"**, Needham, Harper & Steers, 1975.
88. Bartles & Jaymes, **"Frank and Ed"**, Hal Riney & Partners, 1985.
89. Dannon Yogurt, Old People in Russia, Marstellar Inc., 1970s.
90. Volvo, Average Life of a Car in Sweden, Scali, McCabe, Sloves, 1960s.
91. Motel 6, **"We'll Leave a Light on for You"**, Richards Group, 1988.
92. Jell-O, Bill Cosby with Kids, Young & Rubicam, 1975.
93. IBM, Chaplin's Little Tramp Character, Lord, Geller, Federico, Einstein, 1982.
94. American Tourister, The Gorilla, Doyle, Dane Bernbach, late 1960s.
95. Right Guard, "Medicine Cabinet", BBDO, 1960s.
96. Maypo, **"I Want my Maypo"**, Fletcher, Calkins & Holden, 1960s.
97. Bufferin, Pounding Heartbeat, Young & Rubicam, 1960.
98. Arrow Shirts, **"My Friend, Joe Holmes, is Now a Horse"**, Young & Rubicam, 1938.
99. Young & Rubicam, **"Impact"**, Young & Rubicam, 1930.
100. Lyndon Johnson for President, **"Daisy"**, Doyle Dane Bernbach, 1964.

Note: In many cases the Positioning Line or Headline of campaigns is included in the list.

Bibliography

Bibliography

1. **Advertising and Promotion**, George E Welch and Michael E Welch, Tata Mcgraw–Hill, Sixth Edition.

2. **Advertising and Sales Promotion**, S.H.H. Kazmi, Satish K Batra, Excel Books, First Edition.

3. **Advertising Theory and Practice,** C.H.Sandya, Vernon Fry Burger, Kun Rotzoll, A.I.T.B.S., Eleventh Edition.

4. Blogs Give PR New Job by Eric Pfanner, **International Herald Tribune**, 2006.

5. **Foundations of Advertising—Theory and Practice,** S.A.Chunawalla and K.C.Sethia, Himalya Publishing House, 2005 Print Edition.

6. Don't Sexualise Kids: Cameroon by Jane Merrick, **Daily Mail**, London, 2006.

7. Humour in Advertising by **Oppapers.com**

8. India Advertising Agency – India Media Agency Report – 2009.

9. **Profit vs Ethics,** Shankutala Narasimhan, **Deccan Herald**, 2006.

10. **Shop for Social Goods**, Shakuntala NarsimhaN, **Deccan Herald**, 2006.

11. **Teens Rule: Part of the Media World**, Paul Farhi and Jennifer Frey, **Washington Post**, 29 May 2006.

12. Tom Duncan: **Advertising and IMC,** 2005 Edition, McGraw–Hill.